W9-AWN-013

"Koenigsaecker's long and extensive study and application of lean at the strategic and tactical levels make him a foremost authority on the topic. He has a unique and valuable grasp of the tools, process and change dynamics at implementing organizational lean transformation."

—**Stan Askren**, chairman, president, and CEO, HNI Corporation

"Koenigsaecker's story is an inspirational one. In this book, he captures succinctly over twenty years of wisdom about how to lead a Lean transformation."

—**David Fillingham**, chairman and CEO, Royal Bolton Hospital NHS Foundation Trust

"Koenigsaecker hits a grand slam with Leading the *Lean Enterprise Transformation*, and the operative word is "leading"! George drives home the point that Lean is as natural in the touch labor arena as it is in the intellectual labor arena—and leadership is the key to success in both."

—**A.B. Morrill III**, Major General, USAF, Vice Director, Defense Logistics Agency

"Finally, a hands-on, real-world book written by someone who has actually led several lean transformations. My only concern is that my competitors get their hands on this book."

—**Peter Desloge**, chairman and CEO, Watlow Corporation

"Koenigsaecker has been my sensei for over seven years. The lessons he has worked to impart are all contained right here . . . a must-read for anyone serious about lean process improvement."

—**Donald J. Wetekam**, group vice president, AAR Corporation, Lieutenant General (retired) USAF

"Koenigsaecker has written a wise book that goes beyond an explanation of the tools of lean to provide keen insights derived from his three decades of experience on the ground as a lean leader."

—**Alan Aviles**, president, New York City Health and Hospitals Corporation

"Koenigsaecker makes a complex subject simple... a great 'how-to' guide for leaders on lean process improvement based on years of practical experience."

—**Major General Dave Gillett**

"Koenigsaecker's practical, experience based understanding of lean and its implications for leaders of companies is much needed and enormously helpful. He has the credentials to say it like he experienced it, from the same vantage point as thousands of executives and senior managers all over the world."

—**Robert Miller**, executive director, The Shingo Prize for Operational Excellence

"Very few individuals in North America have the level of experience leading change as George Koenigsaecker. This is a great book for anyone beginning their lean journey."

—**Dan Ariens**, president and CEO, The Ariens Company

"Through the lens of his own transformational journey, Koenigsaecker provides readers with a step-by-step primer for building a culture of continuous improvement and offers interesting anecdotes to support his philosophy that a lean culture will always supersede lean tools."

—**Mike Ward**, president, Autoliv Americas

Leading the
Lean Enterprise
Transformation

George
Koenigsaecker

CRC Press
Taylor & Francis Group
Boca Raton   London   New York

CRC Press is an imprint of the
Taylor & Francis Group, an **informa** business

A PRODUCTIVITY PRESS BOOK

Productivity Press
Taylor & Francis Group
270 Madison Avenue
New York, NY 10016

© 2009 by Taylor & Francis Group, LLC
Productivity Press is an imprint of Taylor & Francis Group, an Informa business

No claim to original U.S. Government works
Printed in the United States of America on acid-free paper
10 9 8 7 6 5

International Standard Book Number-13: 978-1-56327-382-7 (0)

Library of Congress Cataloging-in-Publication Data

Koenigsaecker, George.
    Leading the lean enterprise transformation / George Koenigsaecker.
        p. cm.
    Includes bibliographical references and index.
    ISBN 978-1-56327-382-7
    1. Total quality management. 2. Industrial efficiency. 3. Industrial productivity. I. Title.

    HD62.15.K65 2009
    658.4'013--dc22   2009008462

Visit the Taylor & Francis Web site at
http://www.taylorandfrancis.com

and the Productivity Press Web site at
http://www.productivitypress.com

Contents

Acknowledgments

My journey of lean learning continues, but it has been built on the work of many others. Starting near the beginning, it is appropriate to recognize the people of Toyota, who have carefully distilled best practices from around the world, added unique insights of their own, and built a disciplined business system that is the benchmark for how to run an enterprise. The folks who began the work at Toyota, especially Taiichi Ohno, who pulled much of it together, would tell you that the Toyota model is built on a foundation of the teachings of Henry Ford, W. Edwards Deming, those who developed our WWII training methods, and others. And although this is true, the unique insights of Toyota and the company's ability to create a culture that sustains this corporate learning system are truly amazing.

I owe thanks to folks like Frank Petroshus of Rockwell Automotive, who supported the global learning effort that got me started on this path. Also, folks like Steve and Mitch Rales, who bought a company, and then let me experiment with it. And then, my principal *sensei*, three members of Ohno's Autonomous Study Group, who taught me the basics of the tools and principles of Toyota Business System (TBS): Yoshiki Iwata, Chihiro Nakao, and Akira Takenaka.

Perhaps most important are all the associates at Danaher and HNI/HON, who struggled with my efforts to understand and lead in this new, lean world. I also want to thank Simpler Consulting LP for providing me with a mechanism for demonstrating that, with a solid foundation in lean principles, a lean business system can be applied successfully in any work environment—from health care and other service industries to the military.

I would also like to thank three key editors who worked with me on this manuscript: Terry Rousch (Simpler Consulting); Michael Sinocchi (senior acquisitions editor with Taylor & Francis/Productivity Press); and Tere Stouffer (freelance development editor).

Of course, thanks to my wife, Charlotte, and our children, Danaka, Brooke, and Derek, who suffered through long absences while I was on my journey of learning. None of this would be possible without them.

Introduction

I have been involved with the evolution of lean thinking for more than thirty years. Over this period of time, there has been, in some regard, great progress, as lean implementation has moved from high-volume automotive production to medium- and low-volume, nonrepetitive production, to administrative and general support processes, and even to product development and design. Today, lean is evolving into the public sector, particularly the military, and is now rapidly expanding into the healthcare industry.

This book is focused on what I think of as lessons learned from my thirty years of study and application of lean thinking. I have started eleven corporations on their lean journeys while serving as either president or group president. Most of the lessons learned from these companies were the results of multiple trial-and-error experiments, where I implemented a variety of leadership practices meant to manage the change and build a new culture. Throughout this book, you will see a number of examples from clients of Simpler Consulting, a company I helped found more than ten years ago. I have chosen to use these examples because Simpler has a deep belief in the lean principles, enabling sensei to jump into new industries, find new applications for lean, and demonstrate the effectiveness of lean principles.

Over the years, I have had the opportunity to benchmark—both in a corporate role and as a Shingo Prize examiner—more than 100 organizations that have attempted a lean transformation. Many of the lean efforts I have observed are what I would consider to be failures; that is, they have not achieved the results that a few benchmark organizations have shown to be possible and, perhaps more important, they have not demonstrated an ability to transform their culture into a new lean-learning culture that can sustain a high pace of improvement through multiple generations of managers.

That said, the focus on this book is not on lean tools or lean principles, which are covered extensively in other books by Productivity Press. Instead, the focus here is almost entirely on the leadership aspects of a lean transformation. Up until now, there has been no real guideline for leaders to build and sustain a transformational lean effort in an organization. That is what this book offers.

WHAT YOU'LL FIND IN THIS BOOK

The intention of this book is to provide every reader with a practical guide for effective leadership throughout a lean transformation in virtually any organization. The chapters are organized in roughly the chronological sequence that a leader embarking on a lean journey would experience:

- In Chapter 1, I wander through my thirty-year history with the evolution of lean that resulted in the lessons learned that are presented throughout the rest of the book.
- In Chapter 2, I give you several ways of describing lean, to bring us to a common understanding.
- In Chapter 3, I describe the simple, yet powerful, True North metrics used by Toyota and describes how they drive every line item of the income statement and balance sheet in the "good" direction.
- In Chapter 4, I explain the use of value stream analysis at the leadership level in a way that drives the True North metrics. This chapter also explains how to structure successful kaizen events that then improve the value stream.
- In Chapter 5, I discuss tactical organizational steps that are necessary to achieve double-digit improvements in the True North metrics on an ongoing basis. These include the pace of process improvement activity at which you should progress and the support structure needed to sustain this pace of activity.
- In Chapter 6, I examine the development of a corporate assessment-and-review structure that supports the lean transformation. This chapter also introduces leadership tools such as strategy deployment, transformation value stream analysis, transformation plan of care, and so on.
- In Chapter 7, I discuss building a lean culture, which is the least understood aspect of a lean transformation.

A LEAN TUTORIAL

This book does not attempt to show how to use every lean tool; you can find that in many other books on the market. This section, however, provides you with a basic tutorial on lean. Even if you're familiar with the lean tool-box, you may want to review this section because it offers you a summary of the tools that are used over the course of a lean transformation. You also get a valuable perspective on how each tool is used, when it should be used, what it can accomplish, and how it drives the True North metrics.

I organize these tools into a few general categories: top-level tools for executive leadership; tools that principally improve quality; tools that principally build flow; tools that principally improve cost and productivity; tools that support human development; and tools that are specifically used in the area of product or service development. Almost all these tools have a positive impact on the four True North metrics, so I group them under the True North metrics that they tend to directly impact the most. As noted, setting True North improvement goals in the double-digit area will have a positive impact on each line item of an income statement and balance sheet.

Top-Level Tools for Executive Leadership

A few tools are oriented toward the enterprise-level perspective of the transformation process.

Transformation Value Stream Analysis

I discuss in Chapter 3 how value stream analysis can help an organization learn to see waste in its work, and how such analysis can help build an improvement plan. In addition to value stream analysis, there is a tool called *transformation value stream analysis* (TVSA) that takes a top-level view of a corporation (see Figure I.1).

TVSA identifies key value streams at the top level of the enterprise, assesses their performance as seen by the multiple stakeholders in the organization, and integrates this with the strategic plan of the organization. TVSA takes the insight developed in your strategic plan and builds top-level value stream objectives around the strategic needs and direction of the enterprise. TVSA also helps the executive team understand the potential kinds of improvement and pace of improvement that lean can bring to bear on each value stream and how these improvements fit with the enterprise strategic plan.

You will be able to choose a couple of key value streams in which to begin your lean transformation. These will be value streams that are important

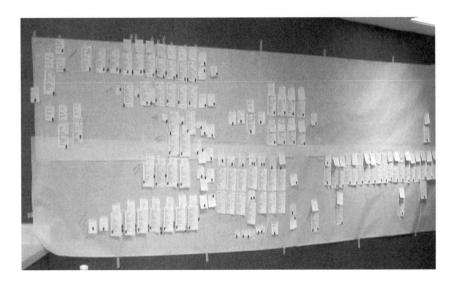

FIGURE I.1
TVSA example.

to the strategic direction of the firm and will demonstrate the power of lean improvement to all stakeholders in the enterprise.

Strategy Deployment

The strategic deployment tool has a couple of other names (policy deployment and *hoshin kanri*), but the tool is essentially the same in each version (see Chapter 6 for details). It is a methodology that takes the enterprise improvement targets and deploys them down through the enterprise, all the way down to the first-level workforce where you find most of the value-added steps. The basic concept is a cascading of goals from one level of leadership down to the next level, where the goals are turned into value stream improvement plans. This part is called *catchball* by the Japanese. It is meant to be an exchange of views and knowledge about the improvement effort between two levels of leadership.

You'll begin to ask the following questions:

- What value streams will we need to work on to achieve the enterprise level improvement goals?
- What pace of activity do we plan to achieve these goals?
- How will we organize to achieve that pace of activity?
- Do we think these goals might be achievable?

Early on, catchball is difficult because the top leadership typically does not have the lean experience to know what results are truly possible. For that reason, this tool is often not implemented until the second year of a lean effort, after some experience about what is possible has been built up in the enterprise.

The process cycles downward through each level of leadership. Ultimately, at the first level of the organization, there is a work plan for improvement activity for each value stream that is targeted for improvement during that year. And then this process cycles back upward until it confirms the corporate improvement goals and demonstrates that the plan will achieve those goals.

The planning phase is typically done once per year and is a learning experience by itself. Then there is a monthly strategy deployment meeting to review progress made (see Figure I.2), issues that have come up, and opportunities for shared learning. Most companies tend to have a monthly meeting to review performance that is financially driven. Although the meeting tunes the company's direction, it is fundamentally focused on variance to a financial plan. What strategy deployment does instead is create a process that focuses the enterprise on fundamental improvement and

FIGURE I.2
Strategy deployment in action.

on learning from the ongoing improvement experience. Just having the monthly strategy-deployment reviews helps get the enterprise thinking about making the work fundamentally better every month, as opposed to the maintenance focus of most monthly review meetings.

Strategy deployment is a very powerful process and a key part of what a leader does to assure progress in the lean transformation. But it is also a learn-by-doing approach that can be clunky in the first year, tends to improve a lot in the second year, and becomes a standard practice in the third year.

A3

Another tool that is used to develop business strategy, but is also used for everyday problem solving, is the *A3*. A3 is the name for an international paper size. Toyota developed an approach to problem solving that is designed to fit onto one A3 sheet. In typical (humble) Toyota fashion, the company did not come up with a fancy name, but just referred to it by the paper size. There are some slight variations in format, but a typical A3 would be similar to the nine-box A3 shown in Figure I.3.

A3 offers a format that forces you to cover all the key steps in considering a problem or an action. If you follow the nine boxes of information,

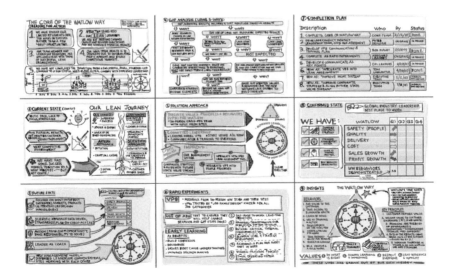

FIGURE I.3
Watlow TPOC.

you will have done a great job of understanding the problem, determining alternative solutions, and learning from the process.

A3 is also designed to use graphical data and sketches to outline concepts. It takes some work to come up with a sketch that will convey a key idea. (I am not good at it personally, but it is remarkably powerful.) Some people cannot really understand easily through words, and these team members will grab onto the idea of the sketch much more easily. And for everyone the "words + sketch" make the idea much clearer and much more memorable.

At first, an A3 seems like a lot of work. But then you begin to realize that it prevents a huge amount of rework that results from implementing ideas that have not been thoroughly thought through. You also begin to see that after the organization is familiar with the format, A3 is incredibly efficient as a communication tool. The combination of words and sketches makes it deeply effective. The focus on covering all key aspects of an issue (the nine boxes) also makes it deeply effective: Getting all the information summarized on one sheet of paper makes it very efficient.

Tools Focused Primarily on Quality

The quality tool kit is an interesting mix. About half of this tool kit is what you would learn in a Total Quality Management (TQM) or Six Sigma effort. And then there is another half that is made up of some unique Toyota contributions.

Five Whys

One tool that is from both sides—originally a TQM tool but taken to an order of magnitude of higher impact at Toyota—is the basic tool of asking why five times. The basic concept is that if you ask why five times, you are about 95 percent assured that the problem you fix is actually a root cause and not just a surface symptom. From personal experience, I suggest that about 90 percent of all quality problems can be solved just by getting the work group together, at the exact time of the quality incident, and then asking why five times. (After the work team asks why five times, you will have found a root-cause solution of 90 percent of daily quality issues. The next 10 percent of quality problems get progressively harder to solve.)

As simple and powerful as this is, most people almost never do it. I have spent much of my career trying to get organizations to use this practice on a daily basis, but by my estimates, the closest I ever got was about 15 percent compliance. This makes for an interesting cultural dilemma: We have, by far, the most efficient quality problem-solving tool and the easiest to learn but it is very difficult to get people to practice it. This characteristic of the implementation of Five Whys is typical of many aspects of lean. It is quite easy to understand the Five Whys (and similar lean tools), but quite difficult to build them into daily behavior.

TQM's Seven Basic Tools

The next step is to typically apply what TQM calls the *seven basic tools*. These are the simple quality tools that include the following:

- Cause-and-effect diagrams (fishbone diagrams)
- Flow charts (process flow diagrams)
- Pareto charts
- Run charts
- Histrograms
- Scatter diagrams
- Control charts

These tools may get you the next 6, 7, or 8 percent of quality problems after asking the Five Whys. One lesson I've learned in my experience is to use the simplest/easiest tool to solve a given problem and escalate to a more complex tool only if the simpler tool is insufficient. As the problem gets more difficult, you find that these tools run out of juice, however, and for the last percent or two of quality problems, you will find that you actually need very advanced tools like Taguchi design of experiments (DOE) to address a problem with many potential causes that are operating simultaneously.

The good news is that if you used efficient tools first, you have solved most of your everyday problems at a root-cause level, so you will never see them again, and this gives you and your team the opportunity to work only on the few really hard quality issues. I use the word "hard" with a specific thought. I don't mean "expensive." You could, hypothetically, reduce costs by solving big quality problems with big cost impacts—in fact, many early

Six Sigma efforts focused only on solving problems with a cost impact of over $250,000. That is a good way to reduce costs, but given that 99-plus percent of quality problems have a cost impact far under that threshold, most of your quality problems remain unresolved. But to become Toyota-like, you can't leave any problems behind, even if you don't think they have a big cost impact. You need to organize to solve these as well.

Poka-Yoke

Toyota also includes a number of quality tools that are unique to its approach. One of these is the idea of *poka-yoke,* or mistake proofing. This is an approach to redesigning individual process steps so that no step can be done incorrectly. Poka-yoke actually designs out even the *possibility* of making a mistake, taking that possibility completely out of a process. A simple poka-yoke example may be found on your car, where the fuel fill opening is intentionally designed to only allow the smaller unleaded fuel nozzle to fit into it. This avoids making the mistake of putting the larger diesel nozzle into it, thus the defect will never occur. Figure I.4 demonstrates a few more examples of this concept. Poka-yoke needs to be part of your total transformation, but it is often not where you start on quality gains.

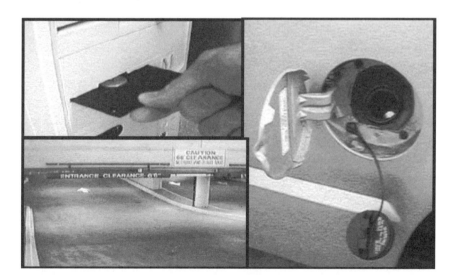

FIGURE I.4
Poka-yoke examples.

Note that if you've done some poka-yoke in your facility, there may be more you can still do. At HON/HNI, we had been working on and meeting a 20 percent annual quality improvement goal. For about four years, the simple stuff worked. But then our gains started to flatten. At that point, we used the motivation of missing our quality improvement goal to drive us to dig into the Toyota tool kit and evaluate how we were using the tools. It turned out that we had done many poka-yoke devices—every site could show one or two. So everyone talked about it as if they really understood it and everyone thought that we had "done the poka-yoke thing." But when we looked at the number of processes that had experienced a quality error in the past year, we found that 99 percent had *not* been poka-yoked. So that gave us a focus for that year. Just expanding the use of this tool across the organization (sometimes referred to as *horizontal spread*) got us that year's quality gain. The leadership lesson is that when folks start talking lean talk, it is good to look closely at how widespread the particular practice is—often what you have is just a sample of use, not a broad application.

The ultimate poka-yoke is a product design poka-yoke. If you can get your engineers to design individual parts and components so that they *cannot* be manufactured or assembled incorrectly at the outset, you will not need to determine later (at higher cost) how to design the process poka-yokes.

Andons

Another Toyota practice is the use of andons. In Japanese, an *andon* is a lantern or light. The idea is to have a signal when there is a potential quality issue. In a Toyota work area, you find andon cords that any team member is allowed to pull, and it sets off a light that is visible throughout the work area. The lights have, in most cases, a yellow light to signal "I think I am running into a problem" and a red light to signal "I have a problem for sure, and I have to stop the work because I am not to pass on a bad piece of work." Typically, the andon light also has a musical accompaniment that makes it easy for team leaders to notice that there is a problem.

There is a dynamic tension in this practice—the team member has an absolute requirement to pull the cord if there is an issue. At the same time, the team leader has an absolute requirement to initiate a root-cause problem-solving effort to assure that the cord is never pulled again for that specific problem. Thus, the andon is not only a way to prevent defective work but also a way to drive problem solving.

Toyota's practice is to keep track of the number of andon pulls per shift. If team members solve enough problems that the number of pulls goes down, Toyota will typically speed up the line a bit, as a way of uncovering the next layer of waste. Like many Toyota practices that have several dimensions to them, one level of understanding of andons is that they are there to keep associates from forwarding defective work. But at another level, andons are a dynamic stress problem-solving tool, and at a third level, they are a way of making the next level of waste visible by allowing the line to speed up. Specific examples of andons, such as those found in Figure I.5, portray other methods used for various types of process abnormalities. These range from a simple five-tier light to more advanced electronic designs.

Quality Checks

In our sixth year of transformation at HNI/HON, we again began to run into difficulty driving our quality improvement goal at the 20 percent pace. At this time we adopted a Toyota practice outlined by Shigeo Shingo that he referred to as *self checks* and *successive checks*. The idea with these two quality checks is to have each team member do checks on critical aspects of their own work before moving the product to the next team member,

FIGURE I.5
Andon and electronic control boards.

FIGURE I.6
Workstations and visual quality check boards.

but also doing a few critical checks of the work that comes to them from a prior team member. Figure I.6 shows an example of workstations with specific quality-check requirements, clearly identified and very visible. This approach helps with the human possibility that someone gets a bit lazy and does not follow their standard work (see the "Standard Work: The Tool That Focuses on Cost and Productivity" section later in this Introduction).

In the next year of our journey at HNI/HON, we found that we really had to do design poka-yoke to take us to the next level. We concluded that the most mistake-proof of the mistake-proof mechanisms were those that were designed into the product. So we initiated a monthly quality review on every product line and then drove to make changes in product design that would not allow this mistake to be possible. The engineers were not excited about doing this, as they thought they were done with the designs. But we found that once we focused on design changes to achieve mistake-proofing, over 80 percent of our quality issues could be designed out, and this focus led to several more years of achieving our quality improvement goals.

Tools That Focus on Flow and Lead Time

In most of the businesses that I have been involved with, I found that we have underestimated the value of faster lead times to our customers. Most lean implementations give a focus on flow as a way to take inventory values down, but the really big gains are pushing your growth rate up two to four times by shortening your lead times by 75 percent on all customer interfacing processes/products.

If you look back at the history of major changes in manufacturing, the Ford assembly line system was a really big one. Taiichi Ohno, who was most responsible for creating the Toyota Production System, often said that he learned most of what he needed to know to build the Toyota System from Ford. There was an element of modesty in this, but also an element of truth, because Ford had built a system that could build a car—from iron ore to dealer—in three days. That was good flow. Of course, we have all heard the story about its limits on variety: "Any color as long as it's black."

Set-Up Times

A core contribution of Toyota and Shigeo Shingo was the idea of reducing set-up time. Most machines (and many intellectual processes as well) have a set-up time—a time during which the work area is made ready for a different product or service. This set-up time is the primary cause of batches in production; in administration, departments function like physically separate silos that connect only through a mailroom, thus creating batches of information flow. An early discovery was that the set-up times, which were thought to be fixed amounts of time for a given machine, were not fixed at all. They could actually be reduced.

Over time, Shigeo Shingo studied set-up times and found that they could be reduced on any type of equipment. He developed a standard practice (often referred to as SMED—for single minute exchange of die, a die being a crucial part of presses that were common at Toyota) to reduce set-up times. When redesigning the HON/HNI office furniture business around shorter lead times, we used this approach to reduce set-up times enough to allow smaller batch sizes to allow faster flow. We found that every time you study a setup, on average, you can reduce it by 50 percent or more. That's right: If you come back a month later, you will find new waste and new areas of improvement and be able, with study, to reduce it by 50 percent or more again. Using this knowledge, we established a program to reduce every machine setup by 50 percent each year for five years in a row. And at the end of each year, we cut our batch size or lead time in half. After five years of this, we had reduced set-up times by about 95 percent and had also reduced internal lead times by 95 percent (we moved from monthly buckets of product to daily ones). We started with a one-month cycle time, the next year it was two weeks, the next year it was one week, the next year it was two-and-a-half days, and the next year it was one day.

Kanban

Another flow tool is *kanban*. Most folks are generally familiar with the idea of using kanban cards to control movement. There are a few leadership issues to consider. One is that setting up a kanban will not directly increase productivity and that kanbans must be maintained—so don't set up a kanban system until you have looked to see whether you can just link the processes without cards. Figure I.7 shows an example of a pharmacy kanban (pull system) for medications that are depleted and need to be replaced before the next anticipated demand for that item occurs.

Kanbans usually are necessary when you have a monumental piece of equipment that many product lines flow through together. You need to set up a kanban to control the flow through the monument. But always keep in mind that kanbans are a form of waste in themselves—they do not directly add value (some folks have set up all kinds of kanbans, and then wondered why they did not become more productive) and they are

FIGURE I.7
Kanban cards used in a pharmacy.

a continuing cost to maintain. In the long term, the goal is to begin to design and build, or purchase, small-scale pieces of equipment that can support individual product-line flows, rather than having these monument pieces of equipment. Equipment builders have a very hard time with this basic idea—it is deeply engrained in them that if a machine of X size is good, one of 2X capacity will be, say, only 50 percent more expensive, and is thus a bargain. Of course they miss the cost of all the work our organizations have to do every day to take flows of various products (different volumes) and shove them through one machine/system. You often find that you cannot get a machine builder to get the idea of small-sized machines, which is why, when you get down to the most basic and smallest machine you need, it is easier to design and build it in-house (see Figure I.8). When you get to this point, you may run into a less well-known lean tool: 3P.

3P

3P (production preparation process) is a tool that helps you invent new processes or designs, and also helps you ensure that a machine design fits with lean system characteristics. The guiding principle with 3P is that every mechanism already exists in nature. True 3P, with its emphasis on

FIGURE I.8
3P: From idea to correct size.

using examples from nature to find new processes and designs, is so different that most organizations need several years of lean before they start the 3P process.

However, the leadership learnings about 3P are rather interesting. After a couple of years of lean at HON/HNI, we started to use 3P to design small-scale machines that fit with lean practices and also to invent new process technologies. The 3P process works in product development, but we had much less experience with it there. We eventually ramped up to where we were running fifteen 3P machine design events every quarter, and had five machine design and build departments building those designs. The general rule of thumb for leadership is that with 3P, you can normally get a given increment of capacity at one-quarter the capital cost of traditional approaches, and you can normally get a fourfold productivity gain. Note that I am reluctant to point out the sort of gains you can get with 3P, as it will probably encourage some to try to do this before they are far enough down the lean journey to have the principles of 3P make sense to them. But for experienced lean firms, 3P is like a second wave of lean. The first wave for manufacturing is to improve the system that was designed around batch or Ford flow concepts. Then, when you have developed a deeper understanding of your flows and of lean practices, you can begin to reinvent every piece of process equipment you have and create a lean production process from the beginning. As you can imagine, this is a very long journey, as you will not redesign and rebuild your whole manufacturing base in a couple of years. But with the faster growth that comes with lean, you will get to the point where you want to do this sooner than you may have thought. And if you go this route, you can build process technology advantages that your competitors cannot match.

2P

The concept of 2P (Process Preparation) is related to flow principles, but without utilizing the ideas taken from nature that are found in a 3P. The concept of 2P is an easier one to grasp than 3P, and consequently can be used earlier in your lean journey. 2P is often used to design flow into the layout of a value stream. For instance, the ThedaCare Hospital Group used 2P to design flow into their in-patient process, as shown in Figure I.9 and Figure I.10.

FIGURE I.9
2P: ThedaCare collaborative care work area.

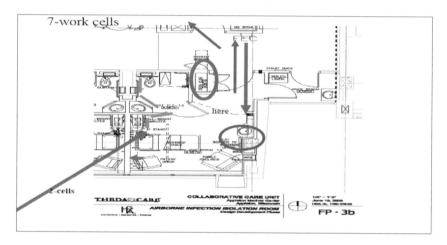

FIGURE I.10
2P: ThedaCare collaborative care layout.

Standard Work: The Tool That Focuses on Cost and Productivity

As you would guess, tools that improve quality and flow also tend to improve productivity and cost. But there is a key tool that is the primary source of productivity gains—both for administrative and production processes. In some ways it is the most powerful and widespread tool in the lean tool kit: It is called standard work (not to be confused with work standards). *Standard work* incorporates a Toyota view of the industrial engineering of work with a Toyota view of flow. It also brings strong focus on the value-adding steps at the work process level. With standard work, you start with the *takt time,* the rhythm of output of the work process: how often do you need a product to come out of the process to meet customer demand, or how often do you need an output of information to meet customer demand. The concept of takt time is the truly unique one, as it redesigns the process around customer needs—whether it is a manufacturing, service, or administrative process.

Standard work then lists every step in the process and takes a quick time estimate of the human work content to achieve that step. While engaging in this process, there is a constant cycle of asking yourself:

- Is this truly a value-adding step?
- Do I really need this step?
- If a customer saw me doing this work step, would he or she be willing to pay me to do it?
- How do I assure quality and safety in this step?

Answering these four questions for every small process step will improve the process. After the work in the process is both improved and documented, the manpower is applied to the process. Starting at the end of the process, you fill each person in the process to a full day's work, based on the takt time and the work content.

One of the unique aspects of Toyota's look at work is that you do not want to *balance work* (see Figure I.11). Balancing hides waste and makes it harder to remove. You want to fill each person with a full day's work, and then leave the last person with partial work (see Figure I.12). One aspect of this is that you are fully utilizing all the human resource in the process, except this last person. And a second aspect is that this person has spare time in his or her day—the goal is then not to fill this time but to improve the work process further so that you can free up this person completely. This partial work concept is another way that Toyota helps to make the waste visible. Figure I.13 shows the improvement impact after a kaizen event has been done.

The outcome of the review is a revised work practice documented in standard work combination sheets. These are posted at the actual place where the work is done. Figure I.14 illustrates exactly how much time it should take for each operational step or task in the process. These sheets are another tool for seeing waste quickly by observing normal versus abnormal conditions.

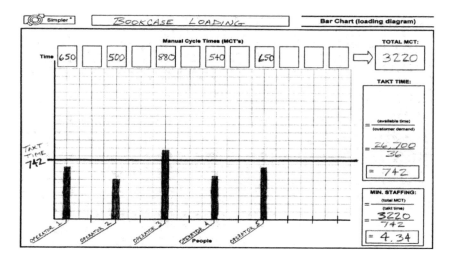

FIGURE I.11
Bar chart showing poor daily workload per operator.

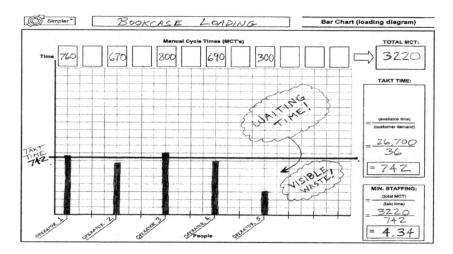

FIGURE I.12
Bar chart showing good daily workload per operator.

When Toyota senior leaders do site visits, one thing that is always reviewed is the standard work practice. Senior leaders look to see whether the standard work combination sheets are posted at each workstation. They then sample a few workstations to observe whether the member is following the standard work exactly as detailed. If the work is being followed exactly, senior leaders then check the dates on the standard work

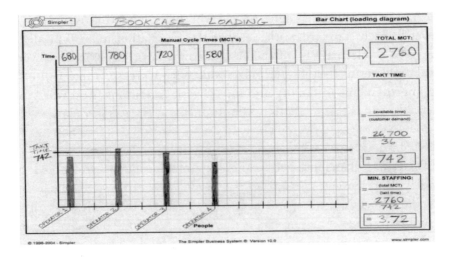

FIGURE I.13
Bar chart showing daily workload per operator after kaizen.

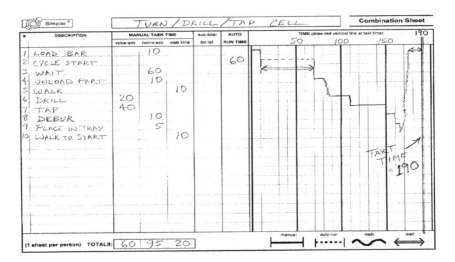

FIGURE I.14
Standard work combination sheet.

combination sheets. If the sheet has not been changed in a long time, there is cause for a discussion about improvement in the work area, because if there had been any improvement since that date, the team leader would have had to update the standard work combination sheet.

Standard work may seem like a simple and mundane tool, but it is *the* key tool to finding and removing waste in any process—administrative, service, or production. Many people who have applied lean tools have never learned standard work, yet it is the foundationstone. Typically a standard work analysis, often done during a lean improvement event week, will result in a 40 percent productivity increase. There will also be improvements to quality and safety/work conditions. And what you typically find is that every time you restudy an area with standard work, it opens your eyes to the next level of waste, and you will find another 40 percent productivity improvement.

At HON/HNI, in our fourth year of lean transformation, we checked the standard work events of the prior two years. In that time, we had run 491 standard work-improvement events (the weeklong, focused variety), and found that, on average, we had achieved a 45 percent productivity gain each time we studied an area. Many of these standard work events were the second or third pass at the area, and each generated about the same average productivity gain. We also evaluated the administrative standard work events that we had conducted, and the average administrative standard work event resulted in an 80 percent productivity gain.

Typically, I expect that real productivity gains will pay for all lean transformation costs within 90 to 120 days. (It should never take more than 120 days for a total return of your member's time, your *sensei*'s [mentor's] time, and your physical redesign costs. If it is not paying back this fast on productivity, you need to reevaluate the quality of your events and follow-up.) Standard work is the primary driver of those productivity gains.

Once an organization has learned how powerful standard work can be, there is a tendency for managers to only do standard work events. What happens when you do this is that you get a large productivity surge, but after a while the surge starts to falter because you haven't improved your quality or your flow. These quality issues then start to disrupt your process, and material or information flow begins to disrupt your process, too. As a crude average, you want to run about one-third of your improvements events as standard work events, and about two-thirds as events focused on improving process quality, improving human development, and building flow (things like establishing a kanban around a monument or conducting a set-up reduction event).

The importance of standard work was driven home to me in the mid-1990s by a visit to Toyota's Georgetown, Kentucky, operations. My principal sensei, Yoshiki Iwata, had also been an important sensei early on to Fujio Cho, who was then president of TMMC (Toyota Motor

Manufacturing Corporation; now chairman of Toyota worldwide). Iwata invited me to visit Cho in Georgetown, which had been in operation for about fifteen years. By this time, I had been a casual student of lean for about twenty years and a serious practitioner for about ten years. I had, by that time, learned many of the tools and concepts of lean, but I was looking for the next breakthrough concept or tool that could take my organization to a higher level of lean performance.

I decided to ask Cho what was going to be his focus of improvement for the next year in Toyota's operations. I was sure that at Toyota's level of experience and sophistication, this focus would be something revolutionary to me. But when I asked Cho this question, his answer was simple: standard work. His point was that there was still much waste in all of their work and that a reemphasis on standard work would allow Toyota to identify and remove this waste.

Tools Focused on Human Development

Human development is the cornerstone of the lean enterprise. The new knowledge you build into your team members becomes your largest off-balance-sheet asset. There is a lot of loose talk about how important people are in most firms, but in a lean firm, this is really true. The key to success for a lean transformation is the continuous restudy and redesign of processes of all kinds of work, and this work is done by your own team members. They will need a sensei to guide their learning for a long time, because there is a lot more to learn than most people could imagine, but the real work of lean process improvement will be the work by your team members. And out of this work, they will not only improve your processes, but also build the knowledge of how to do it. This knowledge becomes your greatest resource as an organization.

Event Participation

Although it is more of a practice than a tool, the use of teams with cross-functional groups of members from your own organization is a key building block of human development. It is through this experience that your team members will learn how to work in a team fashion, but also they will learn the tools/practices/principles and leadership habits that create a massive human resource asset.

5S (or 6S)

Normally, the first tool used in either an administration or production setting is a deceptively simple tool referred to as 5S or 6S (where the sixth S is for safety). It is deceptive because the Ss in Japanese are the basic steps in good housekeeping. They are:

- **Seiri (sort):** Eliminating everything not required for the work being performed
- **Seiton (separate):** Efficiently placing and arranging equipment and material
- **Seison (shine):** Tidying and cleaning
- **Seiketsu (standardize):** Standardizing and continually improving the previous three (seiri, seiton, and seison)
- **Shitsuke (sustain):** Establishing discipline in sustaining workplace organization
- **Safety:** Creating a safe work environment

5S/6S seems too simple to most managers, but it turns out it is a foundationstone for lean. The impact of a 5S/6S effort is obvious to all in the work area. It gets things arranged and organized. And being organized makes the workplace more productive. 5S/6S also makes the workplace cleaner, safer, and less frustrating. These benefits are visible to all and begin to create buy-in for the lean journey to come. In addition, the daily practice of cleaning and organizing your work area takes discipline, and the benefits of this discipline are easy to see, so it is easier to buy into this new work practice, thus getting your lean effort off on the right foot. Given that a lean system is much, much, much more disciplined than either a batch or Ford flow system, building this new sense of discipline is one of the core building blocks of lean. As a leader, you do not want to underestimate how hard it is to get team members who have been free-forming their work to follow a disciplined and standard process.

With lean, you always follow the standard work. You also periodically do a kaizen and test a new way; if it works you adopt it. You always run to each successive standard work practice. This concept is a completely new way of working for most team members. So even though it seems simple, 5S/6S should be your first step; it will earn its way in short-term productivity gains and build a foundation of buy-in and work discipline that will pay off for years to come.

FIGURE I.15
5S/6S: Everything in its place.

After getting geared up for 5S/6S, we also found that after we had 5S/6S'd an area, we typically got a 15 percent average productivity gain from the area. Figure I.15 shows an area that has a high standard of 5S/6S practice in place. At a glance, you can quickly identify anything that is out of place or missing.

Ergonomic Kaizen

There is also a tool that helps you redesign the workplace to fit with ergonomic principles. Often called *ergo kaizen,* this is another tool that builds buy-in and at the same time generates enough productivity to pay its way. Typically, after an area has gone through a 5S/6S effort, an ergo kaizen study will yield another 15 percent productivity gain. And, of course, it will lower workers' compensation costs and improve morale. In fact, as we acquired firms, we made the start-up of a safety program and ergo kaizen the first step of lean integration. Once the newly acquired team members saw how serious we were about safety, everything else went much smoother.

Teian System

There is also a uniquely designed suggestion system that fits with lean. The *Teian system* has its emphasis on developing buy-in to the idea of improvement and on the development of human problem-solving skills, rather than an emphasis on cost savings. In fact, a Toyota operation would typically not put any focus on the savings from a suggestion system for at least three years. The first three years would be focused on building participation (with the idea that if you participate, you will develop a more positive attitude to any kind of improvement and also develop problem-solving/improvement skills that will be of value). For the first two of those years, the focus is usually on getting a higher percent of the workforce that has participated—95 percent being a good second-year target. Then the third year focuses more on increasing the number of implemented suggestions from the average team member. The world-class benchmark (the optimum from Toyota experience) is around twenty-four implemented suggestions per team member per year; they may focus on safety, quality, productivity, or flow.

But keep in mind that it is not a suggestion system but an implemented suggestion system. There is support for team members or small groups of team members to implement their own suggestions, at the same time there is no credit for entering suggestions—only for improvements that are actually implemented.

Involvement is the key. Involvement will lead to changes in attitude as well as the motivation to improve and to building of new skills. Involvement is the goal of the Teian system.

Tools Focused Primarily on New Product Development

It turns out that the tools and concepts that we have talked about in the rest of this Introduction can all be applied to aspects of product development. However, lean product development has a whole additional set of concepts, tools, and practices. This section gives you a sampling of the most effective tools. There are other tools in the lean product-development tool kit, such as modular design, variety reduction, product clinics, etc.

Early Decisions

One of the concepts is the idea of making early decisions. Most companies organize product development projects in a sequential fashion, but then find that late in the project, the team has to start over, because members did not agree on key decisions early on. At Toyota, there are "toll gates" at which the project is not allowed to move ahead unless key decisions are made.

Forced Innovation (or Set-Based Concurrent Product Development)

Another concept is the idea of *forced innovation* in each development project; this is also called set-based concurrent product development. The idea is to assure that innovation occurs, and at the same time assure that the product goes to market on schedule. Normal product development often misses the target date to market, due to rework loops in the process of development (part of what the toll gate process in the preceding section addresses) and also due to efforts to come up with an innovation that throws the project behind schedule. The Toyota practice has a defined time, very early in the development project, at which there is a resource allocation to push improvement to basic concepts in the design. Typically, there will be three alternative designs that will go through an intensive development and test effort in a constrained time frame.

The first alternative will typically be a basic design, with only some modest improvements to the design. This is a design that can be implemented, for sure, within current project constraints for time, cost, quality, and functionality. Then a second, more advanced design alternative with potentially more benefit will also be pushed through a rapid period of experimentation at the same time. And a third, very advanced design alternative that is rather far out will also be pushed through a series of rapid hands-on experiments. If a very advanced design (the third alternative) makes rapid progress and can be turned into a proven concept in the short, constrained period of time, it will become the alternative choice for this development project. More often than not, however, this will *not* be the case. If this very advanced design is a bust, then it is documented (on an A3) for learning, and will then be dropped. If the advanced design (second alternative) shows significant promise but cannot be ready for introduction after this short period of innovation, it is put into a further development cycle and developed to the point where it is a proven design ready for production during the *next* development program. The result is significant innovation, but no delayed product introductions.

Voice of the Customer (VOC)/Quality Function Deployment (QFD)

Another tool used in product development is the voice of the customer (VOC) process. Usually this is organized into a quality function deployment (QFD) house of quality (QFD is a systematic method for translating true customer needs into product and service requirements). The emphasis on understanding the true voice of the customer is the foundation for a good product development effort. The use of QFD organizes VOC data so that it is deployed into design specifications, into process choices, and into after-sale service support.

For most firms, the use of a good VOC process and QFD can make a huge positive impact in development efforts. Most development efforts are run by engineers who know the technology but are usually not allowed to learn much about customers. So we end up with technology solutions to problems that customers don't have. For the typical firm, just getting product development targeted at true customer needs is a huge step ahead and usually involves getting key development engineers to personally visit customers, with an organized approach to assessing their real needs in products and service. When developing key vehicles like the Lexus cars or the Sienna minivan, key Toyota engineers traveled around the country to see how target customers used similar vehicles; they even moved in with target customer families to better understand how they thought about their cars. The point is that you need the folks who know what is technically possible to get into direct touch with the folks who have the needs.

At Jake Brake, back in the early days of my lean journey, we would gather our VOC knowledge, then put together a very broad group of our best and brightest from sales, marketing, design, and production. We would lock them together for a minimum of a week—and sometimes more—and require that they take the VOC and do a paper exercise of deploying it through the whole QFD process. This broad group would be open to lots of alternatives about how to meet the VOC. And by requiring them to go through the whole QFD process before the start of the project, we were able to get most of the early decisions made. After this QFD effort, we would then do a more detailed effort by the assigned project team. But the first one was a real brainstorming effort.

The key is that most companies have huge inefficiencies in development programs, most often because of not targeting the true VOC. We have to force ourselves to spend the time up front, where we can impact the project results without much impact on project cost and time. Think of it this way: The management time spent reviewing development projects tends to escalate as it gets close to introduction (by then it is mostly creating more non-value-added work), but at the beginning of the project, when significant impact on decisions at low cost in time and dollars are available, there is almost no management time spent.

Kano Analysis

Lean always works best as a growth strategy, and one of the best ways to foster growth is to apply a *kano* analysis to your product development efforts. The kano analysis tool looks at the typical product strategy of meeting VOC product-based definitions, and compares it with a product development growth strategy of delighting customers by fulfilling unspoken needs or wants (see Figure I.16). Given that lean typically creates some productivity and margin improvements, it is normally appropriate to begin to refocus product development efforts toward delighting customers (that is, meeting those unspoken needs/wants). And successful VOC efforts are often able to identify these unspoken needs/wants.

Obeya

One other real key tool is *obeya*. This is another typical low-tech Toyota practice. The word *obeya* stands for "big room," and the practice involves the key cross-functional team members all working in the same large room while on a project. (Toyota has found that computer interfaces are not a good substitute for this person-to-person interface.) The value is face-to-face communication throughout the development process, especially among functions that often do not talk to one another.

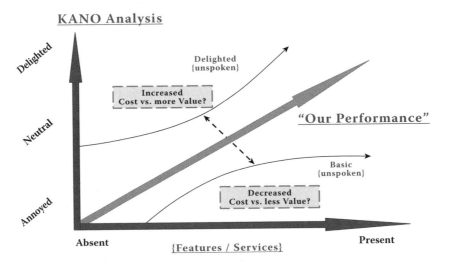

FIGURE I.16
Kano analysis.

FIGURE I.17
Obeya room: Face-to-face communication.

My experience is that communication decreases at the square of the distance that two people are apart (the science behind this was not great, but conceptually it is correct), and in product development, you want to encourage high levels of communication. I've gone so far as to arrange the folks who had the most interfunctional communication difficulty—product engineers and process engineers—with their desks facing each other. Simple but powerful. This concept is known as the *obeya* or the *big room* (see Figure I.17).

Your biggest impacts will come from truly understanding the needs (spoken or unspoken) of customers, connecting the knowledge of what is technically possible with those needs, and then deploying this knowledge into design specifications, process specifications, and service design—at the very front end of the process of development. This is where senior leadership should spend its time.

SUMMARY

I have not covered all the tools and concepts in the lean tool kit, and the ones I do cover I have not explained enough to actually be able to apply them. But, with any luck, you do have a better idea of the range of lean tools and some useful rules about the application of these tools.

1

My Journey of Lean Learning: Eleven Corporate Transformations

The lessons shared in this book represent my learning over the past thirty years about lean—or perhaps, more specifically, about the Toyota Business System (TBS). (Note: I prefer the term Toyota Business System, because it is aimed at the full business. Toyota uses the phrase Toyota Production System [TPS] for historic reasons, but those using that term are almost always talking about an approach to running the whole enterprise.)

Over the years, I have seen many companies attempt to apply the wisdom of Toyota to their enterprises, and I have seen most of them fail. For this reason, I am proud that all eleven firms that I started on the lean journey, as either president or group president (within Danaher Corporation and HNI Corporation), have all stayed true to the path and are still practicing lean learning. Not all eleven are discussed in this chapter; instead I give you a few relevant examples.

Although I would not consider any of these firms to be perfect in their path to Toyotadom, the first Danaher businesses have stayed the course for twenty years, and the first HNI business, fifteen years. No one can claim to completely understand all the elements of success that have made Toyota the model of a well-run enterprise, but at least the results and cultural foundations that were established at Danaher and HNI were strong enough to have lasted.

DEERE & COMPANY

My business career started with Deere & Company, the farm machinery firm based in Moline, Illinois. By the mid-1970s, after I had been with

Deere for a number of years and worked in a variety of areas, I was given a project to assist in a "strategic alliance" with a Japanese firm called Yanmar Diesel. I went through all of Yanmar's production facilities and visited many Yanmar dealerships in Japan. I also had met with Yanmar senior management who, at one point, presented a couple of slides outlining its improvement efforts over the prior three years. I was a student of manufacturing at some level, and I had seen Deere invest 4 percent of sales in capital spending, which generated about 3 percent annual productivity growth. These sorts of numbers were my benchmark, as Deere was the leader in its industry. At Yanmar, however, they noted that they had more than doubled their product range in the prior three years, while at the same time more than doubling enterprise productivity—and they proved it with major margin gains. At first I thought I did not understand the translation, but upon realizing that they meant it, I was astounded. This represented an order of magnitude of our annual productivity gain, but I had not seen signs of significant capital investment in my tours of the Yanmar facilities. A few other Yanmar metrics also were in this same range of an order of magnitude: inventory turns, customer complaint rates, and so on.

Turns out what I saw was an early application of the TBS. After a lot more conversation, it came to light that Yanmar had three Toyota sensei (master teachers) who visited them on weekends, helping change the way they ran the business. And these gains were the results of those long weekends.

Taiichi Ohno was the guy who did much of the pulling together of concepts to create the TBS. He also generated several aggressive change-management practices that have been forgotten by many since then. The Autonomous Study Group was Ohno's Toyota-wide brain trust used to design its system. And these sensei were three of the first five members of the original Autonomous Study Group.

I was blown away by the difference in the rate of improvement on all key performance measures and, to be honest, I was afraid of what I saw. I knew we would need to learn how to practice these approaches if Deere was to maintain its position. After returning to Moline, I arranged for Jim Abegglan, the foremost Western expert on Japanese advanced manufacturing practices at that time, to visit Moline and give a senior leadership review of Just in Time (JIT) manufacturing. But after the reviews, I remember being disappointed: Deere was doing quite well at the time and the net was something to the effect of, "Gee, George, that was very interesting … thanks for bringing him here. But I don't think we would want to try that Japanese stuff in Moline." In contrast to that lukewarm reception, I was hooked on learning about this different way of running a business and continued to read anything I could find on the subject. Unfortunately, there was not much to read in those days and much of what there was to read turned out to be incorrect, written by outsiders trying to describe something they did not really understand.

ROCKWELL INTERNATIONAL

A while later, I was recruited to join the Automotive Operations of Rockwell International. The company was based in Detroit and was a major player in Class 8 (heavy) truck components, including axles, brakes, and drivelines. I took the position, both because it was a promotion and because I thought that being in Detroit—an automotive town that surely had to be doing things the way Japanese automaker Toyota was—I would be able to learn more about what we now refer to as lean.

As it turned out, Detroit in those days was not much more interested in Japanese automotive practices than Moline was. Nonetheless, I was able to get support from Automotive Group management to lead a small team that would benchmark best practices in manufacturing enterprises on an international basis. We were benchmarking against our own business units: Rockwell had the policy of being either No. 1 or No. 2 in the industry. We were in the largest global market; therefore, we were the No. 1 or 2 global competitor, and we assumed we would be the standard of performance.

The team was principally myself and Bob Pentland, who was considered one of our very best production engineering guys. We started spending about three weeks on the road each quarter, visiting firms and benchmarking their performance.

In those days, Rockwell was building the space shuttle, the B-1 bomber, and similar "interesting stuff," so we had purchasing and sales offices around the world, which meant we were able to get into almost any firm we wanted to visit. We went around the world and quickly found that although European firms often developed a unique process technology and built successful businesses around it, they did not operate in any fundamentally different way from ours. But after the first tour in Japan, we began to see a few firms that were radically different. Over three years, we visited 144 manufacturing enterprises in Japan. Some were the big guys, like Matsushita; some were good midsize manufacturers, like Omron; and others were smaller automotive industry suppliers. We toured all the major Japanese automotive OEMs (original equipment manufacturers), and then started to go around their supply base.

What we saw was that about 15 percent of the firms we visited had radically superior performance metrics. We found firms making essentially the same class of product at four times the enterprise productivity, at 90 percent lower defect and customer complaint rates, and with 90 percent less inventory investment. It was hard to believe. At first we were not sure we really understood what we were seeing, but as we kept finding more firms that operated in this fashion, we realized that this was real performance. We also realized that the firms that had this order of magnitude superior performance were all part of the Toyota Group and its extended family of firms. We became believers. Of course, back in Detroit, these findings were just too incredible to be believed, so they were not.

Bob and I were learning about a couple of the basic tools that were used to improve performance—things like better flow and set-up reduction that allowed for lower inventories—but we also could tell that we really understood only the tip of the iceberg. We didn't have many ways to learn more, but during our tours in Japan, we had found a "Japanglish" translation of a book by Shigeo Shingo. In it, Shingo described the Toyota approach as he understood it and in his terminology. Between the local translation and Shingo's rather obscure way of explaining things in the first place, it was a real drudge to try to figure out what he was saying. As we rode trains from one Japanese operation to the next, we read a paragraph at a time and tried to decipher what he meant. Since it was the only thing written about the subject, we worked it hard. We also tried to apply the lessons back in the United States and to experiment in our own operations.

JAKE BRAKE (DANAHER)

After a couple of years, I got the chance to run a company in Connecticut called Jacobs Vehicle Manufacturing Company, or Jake Brake. It turned out that Jake Brake had a great product (engine "retarders" or brakes made for heavy diesel engines), and we were shipping to folks like Cummins Engine, Caterpillar Diesel, and Detroit Diesel. We had good quality, but due to patent coverage, we had become arrogant and unresponsive to our customers. We typically were shipping a month late and in monthly batches of products. We also charged a bit too much for the product.

Shortly after joining, however, I found out that the patents had recently run out. Just to make it a bit more interesting, about this same time, a new company called the Danaher Corporation took over the parent of Jake Brake, Chicago Pneumatic Corporation, in a hostile buyout. There were fifteen companies in total that made up Chicago Pneumatic, fourteen of which lost money, so the new owners, Steve and Mitch Rales, had a special interest in how things were going at Jake.

The performance gap we already had between our delivery and our customers' expectations made me think that we had little to lose by trying to radically change Jake Brake with Toyota's practices. I didn't feel as though we knew enough, but we started anyway. Given the magnitude of our crisis, we started very fast. Most of our associates thought that this approach would fail and that we would kill the company in the process, but we started anyway. Over the 1987 Christmas vacation, we moved all the equipment in the plant into a crude cellular flow. When we started up again in January, we began to see gains. We thought about the gains we saw at Rockwell organizations and the Toyota operations we had benchmarked in Japan and decided to set a goal of achieving a fourfold enterprise productivity target, which means growing enterprise productivity 2 percent every month for six years. As we put in place our new flow, we naturally ended up with something that looked like product line value streams (the linked process steps to deliver a product or service to a customer). We also found that we had thousands of problems to solve: set-up reduction issues, quality issues, tool-change issues, material-flow issues, and nearly everything else. So we started to dedicate problem-solving resources to each of these product line "focused factories," as we called them. By midyear, two critical events occurred:

- The sensei who had worked with Yanmar in Japan retired from Toyota and with some significant encouragement, I was able to convince them that they should adopt us as their first foreign students.
- Steve and Mitch Rales visited and reviewed what we were doing, why we were doing it, and the initial results.

Steve and Mitch had a real estate, rather than an industrial, background but had decided to build an industrial firm based on very high debt levels (typical of real estate investments) and a strong belief that solid, industrial brands (like Jake Brake) would provide stable platforms that would grow the company. In retrospect, this was a good thing: If they had a strong industrial background, they probably would have "known" that this lean stuff could not work, and we would have been stopped in our tracks. As it turned out, they thought the principles made a lot of sense. They were impressed by talking to our United Automotive Workers (UAW) operators about the changes made so far and encouraged us to continue on.

Over the next two-plus years, we continued to learn from our sensei, who would typically visit and coach us hands-on in the *gemba* (workplace) in *jishukin* events (weeklong kaizen events; see Chapter 3) that not only delivered improvements but also taught us the principles and tools of the Toyota Business System. We began to build a culture of continuous problem solving and continuous learning. In these two-plus years, we redesigned these focused factories (or value streams) five times, each time taking them to a new level of performance. Overall, we were able to take our lead times down from more than thirty days to one day, with 100 percent on-time delivery. We reduced quality issues by over 80 percent and also reduced total inventory by just over 80 percent. But most of all, we grew enterprise productivity 86 percent, which was right at our 2-percent-per-month target.

While we were doing this, we were continuing to visit Japan to learn. We were taught the application in the production world, but we began to apply the lean practices to our administrative and product development process, too. For instance, in product development, we were able to quadruple the total new-product output without increasing the resources and get new products to market in 20 percent of the time it took us to do so in the past.

As we organized our learning and taught it to our organization, we came to call it the Jacobs Business System (JBS), because it was focused on more than just a "production system." As we gained traction, our group executive, Art Byrne, began to spread the JBS to the other companies in his group, and it became known as the Danaher Business System (DBS).

In 1990, I was promoted to group president for the Tool Group, then the largest group within Danaher, and began to spread DBS to those operations. I also established a DBS office that helped document and spread the new learning. My role was interesting, as I now had five company presidents who reported to me and who saw themselves as the leaders of their companies, which they were. Yet I wanted each of them to go through this very difficult lean transformation. The change-management issues that come from spreading lean in this kind of structure were much more challenging than getting a single company on path (like Jake Brake), which had been difficult enough. Aside from the messiness of having five corporations with many locations start on a very new way of doing things, all at the same time, we began to get traction and were able over the next couple years to improve our margins by 4 percentage points, which moved the Tool Group from a small loss to a small profit.

HON COMPANY

At that point, I had parents and in-laws back in Iowa who were at the age where steady health issues were starting to occur. It seemed that it would be good for my family to move back there, if we could, to help out with this. In 1992, I joined HON Industries (now HNI Corporation) and started it on its lean journey. I became head of the HON Company, the largest business unit of the corporation, and was able to drive lean practices there. Again, I had my outside sensei coming in regularly to teach my team how to apply the tools, and once again, my role was to manage all the big-time change issues that come up with a transformation of this magnitude. From 1992 to 1999, when I retired from corporate work, the HON Company moved from No. 5 in its industry to No. 2 (growing sales just under 3X through "organic growth"), with momentum toward the leadership position in the industry. Based on the Rockwell benchmarking and the Danaher experience, we set goals for each HON location and each department to:

- Reduce accident rates by 20 percent each year
- Reduce errors and customer complaint rates by 20 percent per year
- Reduce lead times by 50 percent per year until we get to daily production cycles
- Grow enterprise productivity by 15 percent per year

This is a pace of improvement that I would probably not recommend to someone just starting on the lean journey, as it was challenging, to say the least. But on average, we met these improvement goals each year from 1992 to 1999, and it was this improvement (especially the reduction in our customer lead times) that drove our market position change. And it paid off, as we were named by *IndustryWeek* magazine as one of the "100 World's Best Managed Companies" in 1999 and 2000.

In retrospect, the thing that is most encouraging about these transformation efforts is that all of these companies stayed on the path and are still on the path today. Danaher has lean progress that continues in its twentieth year of lean application and that resulted in Danaher's twenty-year financial record eclipsing that of Warren Buffet's Berkshire Hathaway as a financial performance benchmark. HON/HNI also continues with its lean efforts, now in its fifteenth year.

Today I am a private equity investor and am on the boards of five privately owned corporations in which I have investments (Ariens Company, Baird Capital Partners, Simpler Consulting, Watlow, and Xaloy). At Simpler Consulting, I am both a board member/investor and an executive vice president. Needless to say, each company is involved in the evolution of lean practices. The board role has given me another perspective on the issues involved with implementing lean transformations, because a board member is an adviser with no executive authority. This role sort of fine-tunes my powers of persuasion.

I am also on the boards of three not-for-profit groups dedicated to the spread of lean knowledge: the Association for Manufacturing Excellence (AME), the Shingo Prize for Operational Excellence, and the ThedaCare Center for Healthcare Improvement.

SUMMARY

The tools and principles that are the foundation of lean were originally taught in a production setting; the idea to use these same tools and principles enterprise-wide was experimental and evolved over time. The leadership practices discussed in this book are also the result of a variety of real-world experiments. In most cases, for each enterprise-wide practice that I recommend, there were many experiments we tried that did not work very well. Thus, the point of this chapter is to give you an idea of the long learning curve and the basis for the enterprise-wide recommendations and observations coming in the rest of the book.

2

What Is Lean?

What is lean? There are a lot of ways to answer that question, and many of them are correct—which, perhaps, helps explain some of the confusion around the whole subject of lean. In this chapter, I describe lean in a few different ways, to allow you to decide for yourself what works best.

WHAT TOYOTA DOES

The first definition is the one I got to most recently. After benchmarking the operating and management practices of many organizations, it became clear to me that in any dimension of organizational practice, Toyota was at least the coequal of the best in the world. But more important, it was this coequal in *every* practice area or benchmarking area that I investigated. This consistent first-class performance across all aspects of organizational practice is what truly distinguishes Toyota. That is why my ultimate definition of lean turns out to be something like "whatever Toyota does."

I have spent a lot of time trying to find organizations that practice a single business area significantly better than Toyota does. Having failed, I have come to the conclusion that I should always first seek to understand Toyota's practice before choosing a direction. This perspective came to me some years ago, at a time when there was not much discussion of Toyota in the business press. Toyota itself encourages this due to its continual modesty about its own achievements. We will talk about this more in Chapter 7, as this modesty is one of the keys to avoiding what the Japanese call *big company disease*—or more specifically, the arrogance that usually comes with organizational success and is normally the root cause of the eventual failure of the organization. Today, the financial markets are *beginning* to appreciate

Toyota; its stock market capitalization is now more than the next seven largest car companies in the world combined. Yet, the momentum that Toyota has leads me to think that its stock value is an understatement of its true value.

TWO PILLARS

If you ask someone inside Toyota to describe the Toyota Production System—which would be its phrase for lean—you will typically get several simple and straightforward explanations, each of which is totally correct and each of which provides a substantially different perspective. This lack of a clear written description of Toyota's practice is yet another of the reasons there have not been as many imitators of Toyota's practices as there should be by now.

One such description is that lean is really about two *pillars*:

- The concept and practice of continuous improvement
- The power of respect for people

Taiichi Ohno would often harken to the words of Henry Ford, who noted that "our own attitude is that we are chartered with discovering the best way of doing everything, and that we should regard every process employed in the business as purely experimental."[1]

This concept may seem simple, but the hard part is to build a culture that truly lives this concept, every day, in every process. And that culture is purely a people thing. When people at Toyota talk about "respect for people," that phrase encompasses many things, including designing a system that motivates people to want to improve, teaches them the tools of improvement, and motivates them to apply those tools every day. So at one level, all that Toyota does, is simply this: continuous improvement through people.

IDENTIFYING AND REMOVING WASTE

Another definition of lean (and of the Toyota Production System) might describe it as "merely" a practice and process of identifying and removing waste. And of course, this would also be a totally correct definition.

Waste is an interesting word, and the folks at Toyota are working to get us to think about it in specific ways. Ohno, as he was building the system, described seven key wastes, as a means to help his folks learn to "see waste." His seven key wastes were:

- Overproduction (making more than what you need or before you need it)
- Producing defects
- Movement or transportation (this does not actually make the material or data closer to what a customer of the process would value)
- Inventory (the storage of overproduction)
- Overprocessing (the classic inefficiency that we might usually look for)
- Waiting time
- Unnecessary motion

I think the key to the seven wastes is not that it is a magical list of waste, but that it provides a beginning point for you to change your view of work and a starting point for you to see waste in existing processes.

The end result of this review of work steps is to define steps as either *value-adding work*, or *non-value-adding work* (that is, waste). One way of thinking about this is that value-adding steps *transform* something, either material in a production process or data in an administrative process. Non-value-adding steps, on the other hand, tend to move things around, involve rework, and so on.

Two good questions to ask yourself as you look at each step in your work process are: "If a customer saw me doing this step, would he or she be willing to pay me for it?" and "If I did this step twice, would the customer's pay be twice as much?" When you first document a process, you normally find that more than 95 percent of the time spent *and* 95 percent of the work steps do not add value. But it turns out that you cannot remove all the non-value-added steps in a process. Let's review the example in Figure 2.1, taken from the operations of ThedaCare, a regional hospital group based in Appleton, Wisconsin. In this initial state map, there are several non-value-adding steps (shown in the darker shaded boxes) that were identified as opportunities to eliminate wasteful activities. During a first look at a given process, it is common not to clearly see every non-value-added step. In fact, in most of these instances, the real issue is more about not being able to see the waste. This is where having a highly experienced sensei can prove invaluable to your organization.

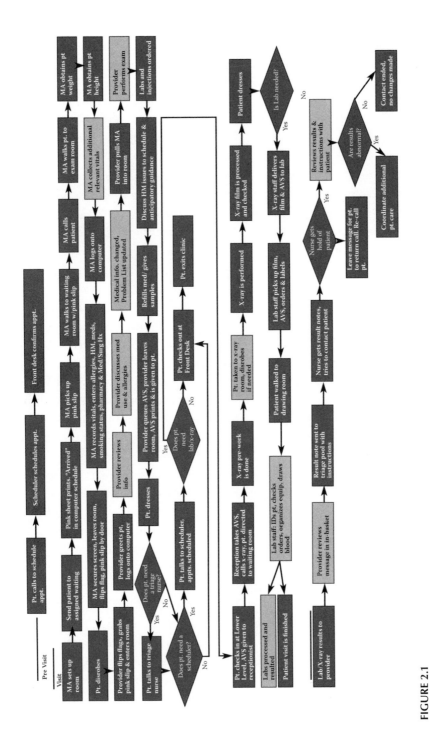

FIGURE 2.1
Identifying non-value-added activities.

If you start to think about waste in this way, you begin to see that the seven wastes are an all-encompassing view of what an excellent organization should be about. You will also find that it is hard to understand this unless you go to the *gemba* (workplace) and struggle with a *gembutsu* (specific process) and the work steps in that process. You have to live and breathe it.

Senior leaders are taught to delegate and not get involved in the details, but the Toyota view is the opposite—senior leaders should know the work and know it intimately. They get to know the work by getting in the work area. With that in mind, the key first step for a senior leader, one who really wants to lead a lean transformation, is to be a team member of an improvement team, documenting a process, step by step, and separating the value-added from the non-value-added steps. There is really no substitute for the insight that comes from grinding through this detailed process assessment, realizing that 95 percent of the steps are non-value-adding, realizing that you can remove half of these steps in a weeklong kaizen event (see Chapter 3). Then realizing that every process in your organization probably looks like this one at the basic work level—and thus the potential for improvement is massive.

Ohno talked about getting leaders to "see waste"—I think what he was looking for was the motivational impact of realizing how much of our hard work, every day, is *not* producing value for our customers and seeing that something significant could be done about it.

Important: Learning to "see waste" is, in my view, the single most important step for any leader to take on a lean journey, and is one you can't do from your office. You need to get into the workplace.

A PROBLEM-IDENTIFYING AND PROBLEM-SOLVING SYSTEM

Another description of lean is to think of it as a system, one that is designed to identify problems, and then resolve them at a root cause level. Given that 99 percent or more of our daily problems are "resolved" at the level of the first symptom, and consequently recur, over and over and over and over, truly resolving them at a root level is a big deal.

Within this description, the key to competitive success is to design your organization to accelerate this spiral of finding and solving problems at the root cause. The problem-solving spiral shown in Figure 2.2 encompasses this idea.

Of course, this description of lean is just as correct as the others. And building a root-cause problem-solving culture in the midst of our daily firefighting is incredibly difficult. Let me say this again: Building a root-cause problem-solving culture is *incredibly* difficult!

American management is trained to hide problems, so before solving them, we first need to learn to see them, to admit that they are even there. Toyota sensei talk about learning to see problems as "golden nuggets," because they are the beginning of your next improvement. But is this how you see problems as they crop up every day?

Thus, getting an organization out of the firefighting mode—that is, to resolve problems at the true root-cause level instead of putting out the fires that spring up throughout the day—turns out to be very hard to do, because it involves changing adult behaviors. (This may be a good time to remind yourself that those tasks that are hard to do often are of significant value. They are also likely to be just as difficult for other organizations, and thus the cultural/organizational learning can create significant barriers to entry from a competitive perspective.)

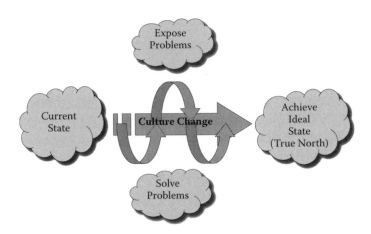

FIGURE 2.2
Continuous improvement: Management philosophy spiral.

SUMMARY

So what we are really talking about with lean is a people-driven improvement system that can improve any work process. What this implies is that the tools/principles and practices of lean can improve any kind of work—anywhere in your enterprise—whether you are part of a corporation or not. The ultimate goal of a lean transformation is to build a learning culture that solves customer problems forever.

The good news is that while your actions are building a new culture, those actions are also leaning all your work processes and reducing waste—reducing defects, speeding response times, reducing manpower requirements, and so on. Done right, this is definitely a pay-as-you-go process. I have yet to see an organization that, by applying lean practices rigorously, is not able to get a three- to four-month (or less) payback on the full costs of implementation, just from productivity gains.

NOTES

1. Henry Ford and Samuel Crowther, *Today and Tomorrow* (Garden City, NY: Doubleday, Page & Company, 1926).

3

Measurement Can Be Easy

One of the phenomena that has amazed me throughout my business career is how many areas we measure when running a business. Back in my Rockwell days, we seemed to measure everything. We had at least 100 key measures that we tracked, reported, and reviewed at every monthly meeting. At some point, it became clear that all this measuring had a benefit (we were so on guard to so many performance dimensions that we rarely went backward in performance), so if our performance metrics would catch the slightest deterioration, we would dig into them at the monthly review meeting. But what also became apparent over time was that, although we put enormous energy into this measurement effort, we could not improve. There were so many metrics that we were never sure which one might have a negative movement if we took action. The result was that we had a measurement straitjacket. We could not deteriorate, but we also could not improve.

UNDERSTANDING FINANCIAL
MEASURES: PERSONAL EXAMPLES

It has taken me a long time to understand which financial measures matter, but here's the evolution of the thinking. When I was at Deere in the 1970s, I was mentored by a number of folks, one of whom, Gene Schotanus, was the treasurer. One of the projects that he gave me was to develop a cash flow forecasting model for Deere, the world's largest producer of agricultural equipment. As it turns out, Gene handled this in a very Toyota-like mentoring fashion: I was handed a significant problem, without much guidance on a solution, and the learning came from the struggle to understand, not from direct teaching. In rough terms, this turned out to have a cause chain that was typical of Taiichi Ohno's Five Whys.

So what causes cash flow to increase or decrease for Deere?

- **First why:** Increases or decreases in inventory or receivables are the initial driver of a change in cash flow for Deere. (Deere financed much of its dealer inventory, so accounts receivable levels were huge—and of course, we had batch production levels of inventory.)
- **Second why:** Sales changes are the primary driver of changes to inventory or receivables.
- **Third why:** Sales changes are primarily driven by changes in farmers' net incomes.
- **Fourth why:** Farmers' net incomes are primarily driven by changes in crop production (although this is somewhat counterintuitive—reductions in crop production increase net income the most because a small shortage drives prices way up).
- **Fifth why:** Weather is the primary cause of changes in farm production in a given year. Unfortunately, as we tried to get to the next why, we started looking at the impact of sunspots on weather and found that we could not crack the code on long-term forecasting of global weather.

Aside from not being able to create a solid cash flow model, this effort helped tighten my understanding of the connections in the elements of the income statement, balance sheet, and cash flow statement.

Another mentor in my Deere days was the head of engineering services, Jim Lardner. He and I often had long talks about how a company could grow productivity, how much was related to economies of scale, and that sort of thing. The idea of productivity as a core financial driver was, therefore, deeply embedded.

TOYOTA'S TRUE NORTH METRICS

As I learned how Toyota measured its business, I became aware of what are often referred to as its True North metrics. These are a select few measures, and if you improve each of them every year, "good things happen." There are four True North metrics: three of them measure business performance dimensions and the fourth (although it is, perhaps, the first in terms of importance) measures human development. The True North performance metrics are:

- Quality improvement (Q)
- Delivery/lead time/flow improvement (D)
- Cost/productivity improvement (C)
- Human development (HD)

"True North" relates to long-term objectives that guide the organization, that is, through generations. So the metric for quality as the True North goal is zero defects. But not only is it zero but it is zero defect in everything—every work process, every day, in every country. Toyota realizes that it may never reach this goal, but it will work relentlessly to reduce the gap between its current state and its True North state every year. And it will do so by double-digit percentages, typically improvements 10 to 30 percent per year for each metric area. And improvements must be made in all four metric areas; if you focus on only one improvement dimension, the others that are left behind will eventually bring your overall improvement to a screeching halt.

Toyota fears complacency. In Japan they call it *big company disease*, the arrogance that comes from success, that leads to complacency, and that ultimately leads to corporate failure. The True North metrics are, among other things, designed to prevent complacency from building. At Toyota, you rarely hear about the celebration of success (they do celebrate, but it's not a major focus), but what you do see is a focus on the remaining gap between where the company is today and its ultimate True North performance. One key result of this approach to metrics is to keep the organization focused on improvement, on closing the gap, and, consequently, on minimizing the focus on "how good we are" and the complacency that comes from this mind-set.

What would be a good True North measure for lead time? Do you recall the discussion in Chapter 1 that a typical process begins with 95 to 99 percent (or more) non-value-adding time and steps? For lead time or flow time, the definition of True North is 100 percent value-adding time. If you have non-value-added time in the process flow, you have a True North gap and a focus for improvement efforts.

Likewise, the True North measure for productivity is 100 percent value-adding steps in the work. Although you might never have a situation in which all waste or non-value-adding steps have been eliminated, you can still focus on improving that process again and again. In fact, I recently saw an interview with a manager from Aisin Seiki, one of the Toyota family of firms. It was interesting to see that after 60 years of lean improvement the company was targeting yet another 10 percent productivity gain for the year. Double-digit productivity improvement, year after year, for over 60 years. We have a hard time imagining it, but we need to learn how to achieve it.

What about human development? Toyota understands that to get continuous improvement in the first three True North metrics, it must have an organization in which everyone contributes to improvement. That is where human development comes in. At Toyota it is not acceptable to only do your work at a very high level of performance; you must also improve your work. To hit double-digit gains in the True North metrics, year after year, Toyota must have everyone in the organization trained in improvement, motivated to improve, and empowered to improve.

The phrase that Toyota uses to describe this is that they must practice *hitozukuri* before *monozukuri*—roughly, "we build people before we build cars." This may seem obvious, but how often have we put the emphasis on building our human resource in order to get the business results we strive for? A lean measurement practice must include the pursuit of these four True North measures.

HOW HIGH IS HIGH?

As discussed in Chapter 1, when I started at Rockwell, there was growing general interest in benchmarking, so we set up a small team to try to benchmark global manufacturing enterprises and measure the drivers of financial performance—trends in quality, cycle time, and productivity/cost improvements. Leveraging Rockwell's global presence, we were able to benchmark selected firms around the world. Eventually, we identified about twenty Japanese firms that showed a radical difference in the driver measures of improvement and financial performance. They all turned out to be affiliated with Toyota in some way. We did some pretty solid

	"Batch" System	"Toyota" System (Lean)	
Inventory Turnover	3x	30x	Cash generation
Customer Complaint Rate	10,000ppm	100ppm	turns company into
Customer Lead Time		−95%	a growth company
Space		−90%	
Productivity	1x	4x	Margin improvement 2 pts/yr for 6 yrs

MOST DON'T REALIZE HOW HIGH "HIGH" REALLY IS

FIGURE 3.1
World-class benchmarking.

digging—down to measuring cars in parking lots to confirm employment levels—and found some amazing differences for these firms. Figure 3.1 summarizes the differences in core metrics (note that, at that time, we did not understand that human development was considered a core metric, which is why it does not appear in Figure 3.1).

There were a number of shocks in the data. We believed that because Rockwell was the global market share leader, our business units would be benchmarks. Yet, in every case, we found a business making very similar products with radically better core performance. In the area of quality performance, we found benchmark organizations that operated at two orders of magnitude superior quality. That is, if we were at 10,000 defects per million, they would be at 100 defects per million. In the area of flow time, the benchmark firms operated at one-tenth to one-twentieth of our typical flow time, which meant they received the benefits of much lower inventories and superior customer response.

The greatest surprise turned out to be in the area of productivity. We hoped that this improvement approach might increase manufacturing productivity by 40 percent and that would have been huge. But what we found were firms operating at 400 percent of our productivity levels—an order of magnitude (ten times) higher than we expected. In fact we found some businesses that operated at 500 percent of the productivity levels of our global leaders. We were completely amazed that the administrative departments also showed these same general levels of productivity. If a business was the same size as ours, we had 100 people in accounting working on accounts payable compared to their 20 or 25. These numbers held true throughout these true benchmark businesses. We also saw that these Japanese firms focused on improving their core processes in all these staff or administrative areas; in other words, they were applying lean concepts in administrative areas that were similar to those they were applying in production. One note, however: Most administrative employees are not used to being measured in any of the True North metrics. They may receive feedback in one or more of these metrics, but they are probably not being truly "measured." As a result, they likely will be uncomfortable with that notion, at least at first. See Chapter 7 for more on building a lean culture.

So we learned that we did not need to reduce our defects by 50 percent, but by 99 percent. We did not need to cut our lead times in half, but cut them by 90 or 95 percent. We did not need to target growing our productivity by 40 percent, but rather by 400 percent and we needed to do it across all our work—every job and process in the firm. The task was much greater than we imagined, but the payoff was also much, much greater than we imagined. We learned how high "high" really is!

Today, there are few executives who are thinking of making a decade-long journey to grind out improvements of this magnitude. And even fewer really see that this magnitude of improvement has to take place in every aspect of work—from product design to collection of receivables.

Lean is a transformation that builds toward a continuous improvement culture, not a "program" that's designed to make tactical gains. Lean can certainly help as a short-term tactical tool, but the big gains are in the creation of a continuous improvement machine inside your own organization that drives both personal and organizational growth. That could be your legacy to future generations.

At Jake Brake, we knew we should be thinking of a fourfold productivity gain, but we were not sure how long it would take to get there. So we set a target of achieving this goal in six years. The six-year mark was somewhat random, but it gave us an easy monthly target. If we increased productivity at the full enterprise level by 2 percent per month, every month, in six years we would slightly beat our fourfold target. As Figure 3.2 shows, we were irregular month to month, but trended on the 2-percent-per-month rate until well into the second year. Then we hit a recession in the heavy truck industry, and

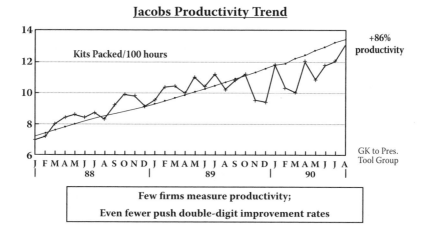

FIGURE 3.2
Lean conversion impact: productivity.

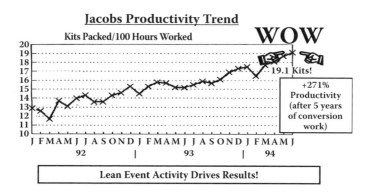

FIGURE 3.3
Lean conversion impact: productivity.

our volume dropped 30 percent. But by the end of the first two-and-a-half years, we were back on track at just under our trend line for 2 percent per month. At that point I became group president of our Automotive Group and undertook the lean journey with multiple firms in that group.

A few years later, my successor at Jake forwarded to me the productivity trend chart in Figure 3.3. This chart shows a couple of interesting things. If you look at the start date and the starting point productivity, you can see that after I left, there was about 18 months with no gain. The management team was not totally committed to the lean path—neither the activity of kaizen events nor the discipline to drive results. But after a time, the team realized that all the metrics had flattened out, and they restarted their lean journey by running weeklong kaizen teams throughout the enterprise. And in the next two-and-a-half years, Jake got back on the same productivity growth curve of 2 percent per month.

At this point, after five years of working the process, productivity was up over 270 percent, and the fourfold goal was looking possible. And by the tenth anniversary of Jake's lean journey in 1998, the company's productivity was over 470 percent of its starting point productivity.

In addition, as productivity was growing, lead times and quality were also improving. As we increased our flows and solved the problems that were impeding productivity, we found that our indirect measures of quality—scrap and rework—were going down, as reflected in Figure 3.4. At first, these gains were an indirect benefit of dropping non-value-added steps from the process; by eliminating these steps, we eliminated the possibility of an error. By the end of the second year, however, those indirect benefits slowed down, and we actually had to begin quality problem-solving to maintain our trend. Overall, by the end of the first two-and-a-half-year period, we experienced an 80 percent reduction of quality issues.

Lead time was a key focus of our improvement efforts. As we started the lean journey, we were shipping in monthly batches of product, and we averaged being more than a month late (see Figure 3.5 for a look at the trend). Our customers, firms like Caterpillar and Cummins, were trying to run their engine production lines, and our delivery performance was

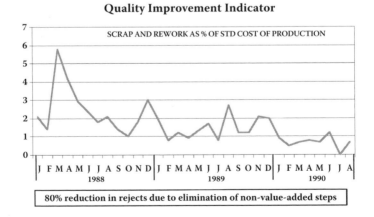

FIGURE 3.4
Lean conversion impact: quality.

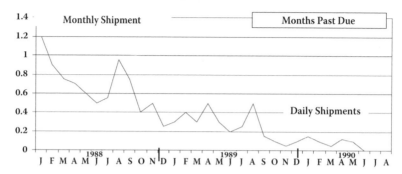

FIGURE 3.5
Lean conversion impact: delivery.

causing chaos. So we made a first pass through all our production value streams (see Chapter 4) and cut the total lead times about in half.

This took about six months of terrific effort. After that, we started through all our value streams again and cut about half the remaining lead times. After that, we started over again, rearranging our equipment and restudying every production process for the third time and taking out about half the remaining time. We did this two more times in the first two-and-a-half years, so that we went from one-month batches, to two-week batches, to one-week batches, to two-and-a-half-day batches, to single-day batch sizes. Thus, by the end of year two we were on a daily cycle, building every product every day, with one day of production lead time.

It took us six more months to get 100 percent on time with one-day customer lead time. In other words, Caterpillar could then call a team member in a cell, let him or her know how many brakes were needed the next day, and the brakes would be shipped within 24 hours—100 percent of the time.

If all these numbers seem a little hard to believe, take a look at Danaher Corporation's application of lean since the first Jake Brake efforts in late 1987. What you see is that the application of the Danaher Business System (DBS) to the core businesses, and then each new acquisition, has led to compounded sales and earnings growth of roughly 25 percent per year, with a high level of consistency. This is the best track record in corporate

America; it is superior to Warren Buffet's Berkshire Hathaway, GE, and so on. *USA Today* reported in 2007 that the Danaher rate of return on a share purchased in the early days at Jake Brake is over 44,000 percent! As always, consistent leadership is critical. Larry Culp, Danaher CEO, was involved with the application of DBS at Danaher from its early days, and he continues to provide strong leadership for the application of DBS at Danaher.

THE FOUR TRUE NORTH METRICS IN DETAIL

Now let's dig into each of the True North metrics a little further.

Quality Improvement

Quality improvement is like mom and apple pie. Everyone is in agreement that it is good. But the reality is that many companies do not seem driven to improve quality. Because most senior leaders have more of an orientation to the income statement and balance sheet—the pure financial metrics—I find it useful to connect them. One study that had a great impact on my view of quality was the *PIMS Principles* by Buzzell and Gale,[1] who studied a wide range of business strategies and practices in about 300 firms seeking to find strategies that always worked. After an exhaustive study, they found two strategies that always correlated with high return on investment (ROI). One was high market share. This is very well known. It's the principle behind only acquiring the No. 1 or No. 2 firm in an industry if you do acquisitions. Basically, what they found was that higher market share almost always was correlated with higher ROI. But then they found something else. They found that higher quality, as perceived by their *customers*, always correlated with higher ROI.

As you move from right to left across Figure 3.6, you are going from low market share to medium market share to high market share, and the bars for ROI level all increase as you go from right to left. However, as you go from front to back on the chart, you are moving from inferior quality, as perceived by your customers, to median quality to superior quality. And as you go up the quality scale you go up in the ROI scale, no matter what market share level you are at. If, for instance, you are a low-market-share firm, but you have superior quality, you will generate an ROI of 20 percent,

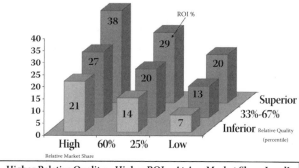

FIGURE 3.6
Lean conversion impact: ROI.

which is a respectable return. And if you are a high-market-share firm with superior quality, your ROI goes up to 38 percent—a great rate of return. So no matter what your industry position today, superior quality will generate the best returns. So with that as your frame of reference, you can think about targeting double-digit quality gains—forever—realizing that this is a great business decision.

Another look at quality and how to focus on it comes from the Technical Assistance Research Program (TARP) study. In this study, researchers found that, on average, "of customers who have been disappointed by defects, malfunctions, or other basic quality problems ... 90 percent go away without saying anything, and do not return" and 85 percent of those also tell "at least 9 other people of their dissatisfaction. ... the other 15 percent voice their dissatisfaction to at least 20 other people."[2] I have often found product engineers waiting to accumulate enough customer complaints before they think a problem might be worth looking into. But if you do the math, for every complaint you hear about, you already have something like ten real quality problems and 130 potential customers who have been warned about your quality issues. This is why the Japanese quality gurus used to tell their students to treat each quality issue as a *golden nugget*; it represents an opportunity to improve, and it also represents the tip of the iceberg of the quality issue in question.

On the positive side, well-known management consultant Paul Bender found that "the cost of turning an existing customer into a repeat customer is one-sixth of the cost of acquiring a new customer." So quality improvement is the lowest cost sales and marketing effort you can undertake.

Continuous quality improvement is a growth strategy, and lean is best thought of as a growth strategy first and a cost improvement strategy second. Lean is much more powerful when you approach it that way.

Delivery/Lead Time/Flow Improvement

When most executives think about lean implementation gains, they go right to the reduced inventory levels that can result. Although this concept is true enough and is an appropriate measure to target, in itself, inventory is just the tip of the flow iceberg. The iceberg is really the benefit to customers of having a responsive supplier. Structural improvements to delivery time/lead time/cycle time/response time, are usually not seen by executives as being of significant value. In almost every organization that I have seen, this increased responsiveness has been of huge value to customers and is a primary driver of top-line growth.

In *Competing Against Time*, George Stalk and Thomas Hout[3] reviewed the impact of time cycle compression (that is, flow) on business growth. As a general rule, they found that reducing lead times to customers by three-fourths resulted in a firm moving to a growth rate that was two to four times the industry growth rate as represented in Figure 3.7.

So if you are in a 3 percent growth industry, by shortening your lead times you can usually move to a 6 to 12 percent growth-rate business. The financial leverage of this kind of growth—especially when combined with

Company	Business	Lead Time Difference	Growth Average
Atlas Door	Industrial doors	66%	5x
Ralph Wilson Plastics	Decorative laminates	75%	4x
Thomasville	Furniture	70%	2x

Lean can reduce lead time of all customer sensitive processes: Product Development / Application Engineering / Order Entry / Corrective Action

FIGURE 3.7
Reducing lead time by 75 percent: Growing at two to four times the industry rate.

other lean improvement dimensions—is tremendous. In the 1990s, HON moved from No. 5 in the office furniture industry to No. 2 by applying these lessons of short lead time, increasing their organic growth rate from the 4 percent range to over 12 percent. At Watlow Electric, which makes semicustom heaters, this concept was applied in one of its business units, a unit that almost always needed to develop a unique design variation for a particular customer application. At the start of its journey, Watlow expected to grow productivity significantly and wanted to focus its lean efforts as a growth strategy to utilize the human resource it expected to free up. Consequently, instead of just working on production lead time management, Watlow decided to start with its earlier customer-facing processes. What this means is that the industry used about a month to respond to the initial quotation request. If this was accepted, there was typically about a month to prepare engineering drawings that could be reviewed by the customer. At that point, it would generally take about another month to build a prototype that the customer could inspect for final approval. Win rates were typically in the 15 percent range for the whole process. The initial lean effort focused on analyzing each of these processes—quotation, application engineering/drawing, and prototype build. The initial target was to study each process three times. It was expected that each complete study of each of these three key processes would reduce the process steps about 50 percent and reduce the process time about 50 percent. Then as soon as this was done, they would be restudied to take the next 50 percent out of steps and time. Then they would be restudied a third time to get 50 percent of what was left to assure that they could always respond with at least 75 percent less time than the competition on each step. So in rough terms, each process went from a monthlong effort to a weeklong one. Now think about the customer engineer who is trying to get her project done. She has more than she thinks she can do (if it were not this way, we would think we had too many engineers, right?) and is probably behind schedule already. So she sends out a request for quote (RFQ) for the special heater that she needs. And a week later, she has a quote back from Watlow. Since she has not seen any other quotes yet, she tells them to proceed. And then a week later, she has the engineering drawings from Watlow. She has still not seen a quote from anyone else, so she tells Watlow to make a prototype. And a week later, she has a prototype from Watlow, and she still has not seen an initial quote from anyone else. Given that Watlow is a known qualified vendor, it is almost a slam dunk that this engineer's business will be awarded to Watlow. In actual fact, in the first year after putting this in place, this 3 percent growth business went to a growth rate of over 15 percent and it was time to get production lean work cracking to handle the volume.

It is amazing to me that this is not the normal response of an organization. For instance, the fastest growing industry for application of lean today is healthcare, and doctors are always surprised to learn that "respondents said they would rather drive further, pay more, and even switch doctors, if it meant faster service."[4] Yet it is always a shock to healthcare organizations that speeding up the flow of patients would make a difference.

Also think about the cross impact of flow times on other areas. You have seen that faster flow is something that can grow a business. Now consider the impact of flow on capacity. If the work flows, you need less of almost everything. One example is in the Royal Navy, which has done a complete first pass of lean to one of its aircraft carriers, HMS *Illustrious*. By studying and redesigning every process—from how it builds up weapons, to how it ties down planes, to how it prepares chips in the galley—the Royal Navy was able to increase the flow of aircraft by two-thirds, which means it was able to sustain about 70 percent more planes in the air compared to its historical performance. In this case, the lean effort almost gave the Royal Navy a free aircraft carrier—ship, crew, planes, and all, just by getting things flowing. That is over a billion dollars of capacity. Commander Alan Martyn of the British Royal Navy (now retired and working as a Simpler sensei) led the lean transformation efforts aboard HMS *Illustrious*. Or take ThedaCare, a leading hospital organization on the lean journey. It used lean tools and practices to fundamentally redesign the way the hospital operates at the patient interface. The net of this redesign was that the patient flowed through the procedures needed with fewer disruptions or waiting. This resulted in a reduction by approximately 80 percent in errors impacting the average patient, a reduction in time per patient stay of approximately 30 percent, and a reduction in average cost per patient stay of over 30 percent. So flow not only achieved higher quality and higher patient satisfaction but also reduced cost by over 30 percent and also increased hospital capacity by approximately 30 percent. This theme will recur—the synergy from lean working together in multiple dimensions of True North performance.

The point is that the True North metric of delivery/lead time/flexibility can be a great driver of growth. Like continuous quality improvement, lead time improvement is like a secret weapon—it shouldn't be, but it is.

Cost/Productivity Improvement

If you look at the income statement of most firms, there are really only two categories of cost that make up over 90 percent of the total. They are (1) outside purchases and (2) costs driven by the number of people it takes to run the business. Most analysts focus on the outside purchases, because that is usually the largest category. In most cases, however, although outside purchases is the single largest cost area, it can be very difficult to create competitive advantage in this area.

Outside Purchases

Much of a firm's outside purchases (things like steel, plastic resin) is driven by global market commodity costs and is thus set for all players. If you have engineered components that are unique to your products (fuel injectors in cars, casters for seating manufacturers), you usually find that these are produced by industry specialists who sell to all your direct competitors. It is very hard to get such a supplier to embrace the challenge of true lean transformation. In Japan, Toyota usually has an ownership stake in key suppliers and often uses retired Toyota executives to run the suppliers (as the supplier folks say, the newly retired Toyota executive "descends from heaven" into their chairmanship). Outside of Japan, where it rarely has the stockholding and executive leadership alignment, Toyota has found it very difficult to get supplier leadership to embrace its system. My own rule of thumb is that at any point in time only one CEO in twenty is ready to undertake the hard work and risk of a true lean transformation. So you can spend a lot of time trying to get suppliers to get on path and end up being pretty unsuccessful. On top of that, if you are successful, you are as likely to see the improvement results used to grow your supplier's business with your direct competitors as to grow your businesses, thus minimizing the competitive advantage of improving your supply base.

People

If you look at all the line items on your income or cost statement, 90 percent of the ones *other* than outside purchases are determined, over time, by the number of people it takes to run the business. I was not at Rockwell for very long before the car business went through a cyclical meltdown and we lost half of our business and, consequently, had to cut half of all of our costs. We struggled to try to figure out how to reduce the cost of everything—postage, telephones, computers, and so on. Then we saw that all of these were really a function of the number of people in the business. Although the lesson came from an ugly downsizing experience, the lesson was that if we could grow but *not* add people, we not only saved the visible people cost of wages and benefits but also kept down the costs of office space, more telephones, more computers, the size and number of conference rooms, and so on.

It is hard to find anything that is not driven by the number of people employed in the business. So it dawned on me that the key driver of internal cost is productivity and that productivity determined over 90 percent of our internal costs (our controllable costs; the costs that really determined our value-add and our competitive differentiation).

Although we talk a lot about productivity, few senior managers spend much time trying to understand how to measure it. And very few organizations are serious about setting improvement targets for productivity and driving to meet or exceed them. And yet productivity is the single major controllable cost driver that can determine long-term competitive advantage.

Thus, the value-adding cost of almost all organizations is driven primarily by its productivity. Outside purchases do not usually distinguish competitive differentiation; instead, it is what you do with your value-adding costs—your people—in transforming your material or information that determines your value-added effectiveness and competitiveness. That is productivity.

Think of it this way: The basic concept behind all productivity measures is output per input. The output is your key value, whether it is brakes produced or patients cured or sustainable sortie rates for an aircraft carrier. The input is human resources—always. You usually do not have to worry about how much each person is paid, but instead just total the hours of human resources that it took to produce one unit of output. For instance, when I worked at Jake Brake, we counted all salaried folks as 40 hours of input per week and all hourly folks at actual clock hours. We felt it was more important to obtain an enterprise measure and that it included everyone in the organization, than it was to count the difference in rates of pay per person. So our productivity measure was hours per engine brake.

As another example, at HON we had product mix to contend with. We were trying to compare business units that made veneer desks, with others that made chairs, and others that produced metal files. In that case, we used the dollar value of product as our output and used hours as the input. The measure turned out to be *X* dollars of sales per member hour. Then we maintained a file of the original unit prices, so that price increases or decreases did not look like productivity gains or losses. In the end, it was a unit measure.

As an executive, you will find that you can get buy-in fairly quickly for improvements to both quality and lead times. But you will find significant roadblocks to improving productivity. After all, to get real productivity gains, you have to redesign the day-to-day work of people, and that is big-time change management.

A rule of thumb is that if you spend, say, 30 percent of your time driving your lean improvement effort, the makeup of that 30 percent may look like this:

- 10 percent of the total to get the organization on path for quality goals
- 10 percent for lead-time goals
- 10 percent for human development goals
- 70 percent to get on track on productivity

Senior managers are typically not used to measuring productivity and have little experience at improving it, so that means learning new practices and new behaviors, and that's not easy. What's more, most administrative staff has never been measured on productivity—and does not want to be!

Toyota has a manual it prints for the leaders of its key suppliers. In it, Toyota notes, "Productivity: it's a matter of life and death ... companies that are more efficient than their competitors in providing customers with high-quality goods and services will thrive. Companies that are less efficient than their competitors will perish." Experience has shown that although quality and lead times can provide growth, productivity is key to improving margins.

Human Development

Behind all the True North metrics is the concept of people studying their work and improving it on a regular basis. So you have to start with the people side. As the expression goes, "The hard stuff is easy, and the soft stuff is hard." Building a culture of continuous improvement to support a lean transformation is a big job. As Toyota says, "We build people before we build cars." I devote Chapter 7 to the human development/culture side and the key leadership behaviors that support a lean learning culture, but for now let's just start at the beginning for an organization undertaking transformation.

First, the organization needs to learn new lean tools, learn new lean work practices, and build buy-in for the whole change process. If you had folks who already knew all the lean stuff, they would be doing it in their work and it would be spreading. But they're not. So, in spite of much talk about lean, you should expect very little true knowledge or experience from those in your company.

The key building block of lean learning, lean buy-in, and lean results is personal, full-time, participation on an improvement team. Toyota spent a lot of time trying various ways to get "results + learning + attitude change (culture)." In the end, it found that a *jishukin* event, a weeklong focused effort was the most effective way, and perhaps the only way, to achieve these three kinds of impact: financial results, opportunities to learn, and cultural change. A typical weeklong improvement event involves a team of six to eight people who focus *full-time* for a week on improving one basic portion of a value stream.

The few truly successful lean transformation efforts you can benchmark are characterized by the use of weeklong improvement efforts. For senior leaders, there is no substitute for actually seeing waste with their own eyes. It is one thing to talk about lean, but it is a whole different thing to dig into a work process in their own organization and identify all the value-added and non-value-added steps—and seeing that 95-plus percent of the operation is made up of non-value-added time (in other words, waste). This personal experience—realizing what waste really looks like (and that there is lots of it around)—is the primary motivator for leadership to drive improvement.

Being an event participant also teaches new tools and practices of the lean world. A few years ago, Toyota in North America did a *hansei* (a deep reflection) to assess its progress on realizing the Toyota Way in its North American businesses. After all, they have been selecting folks to work in that way and training them to do so for more than 25 years. The result of the hansei was that there was serious concern about the depth of under-standing and commitment to the core of the Toyota Way. The corrective action was a refocus on the use of jishukin events. Many Toyota leaders had thought of them as something that generated improvement but they had lost sight of the power of jishukin for learning and building the culture.

For this reason, during a lean transformation, a key metric in the human development area will be event participation. The goal is to get breadth (for buy-in) and depth (the depth comes from people who get over a hundred events of experience and come to deeply understand and believe—these people are your future sensei, or master teachers). Statistical studies have shown that after two event experiences, there is a high level of buy-in for the overall process of lean transformation. So an organization should try to get as many people to experience two well-run events as soon as possible.

There are other metrics in this area; for instance, safety would be a core metric. But the one that will be new to the organization will be the accumulation of learning and culture change experience that comes from the jishukin implementation event.

LINKING THE TRUE NORTH METRICS WITH FINANCIAL MEASURES

Let's try to link the four True North metrics with our usual financial measures. First, think through the key line items in an income statement:

- **Sales:** In a lean transformation, the top line is driven by quality improvements, lead time improvements, and by improvements in the new-product-development process.
- **Cost of sales:** Cost of sales is driven primarily by productivity gains. A doubling in productivity results in a halving of all people costs. This may take several years, but it will happen. And it will be big.
- **Sales, general, and administrative costs:** The vast majority of this cost is made up of people costs. When you double productivity, you cut those costs in half.
- **Financing costs:** As lean impacts the balance sheet in favorable ways, you see your debt decline or your marketable securities rise; either way, your financing costs go in a good direction.

Now for a quick look at some of the balance sheet impacts:

- **Working capital:** With increased inventory turns, you find that working capital required to support a given sales level is lower. If you manage the process, it is also possible to take advantage of some of your lead time improvements to get faster payment terms from your customers, also decreasing working capital required.

- **Fixed capital:** As you build flow, you find that existing equipment and buildings can produce much more volume. A typical lean firm has half the capital intensity of a normal firm in its industry; and advanced lean firms, which use things like 3P to reinvent their processes in a lean format, can run with one-quarter of industry norms for fixed capital requirements. (See the Introduction for more on 3P.)
- **Debt:** Debt is reduced as you free up working capital, but it is also reduced as you increase your net margins and use this to pay down debt. One manufacturing firm with which I have been involved increased productivity by more than 30 percent (enterprise-wide) in its first year of lean and this turned into 6.9 points of net margin gain, which in turn allowed the firm to pay off its leveraged buy out (LBO) levels of debt in less than three years.

There are two things to note here. One is that by driving the four True North metrics, you can impact all these income statement and balance sheet line items, together, in the right direction. The other thing to consider is the synergy of doing all this at the same time. It is not unusual to see ROI measures go up by multiples as you gain synergy from balance sheet and income statement impacts. An example of this synergy can be seen in Figure 3.8, which shows the results of the Heatilator business unit of HON/HNI Corporation. Stan Askren, current CEO of HNI Corporation, was president of the Heatilator business unit during this period of time.

The intense focus in the True North metric areas has shown up as a positive financial benefit in each of the categories depicted in this chart. Note that although the True North metrics have all been improved by double-digit levels, all the financial metrics have improved by triple-digit levels. All these results can be traced directly to the cumulative gains from lean improvement activities, which have now become quite evident in the overall financial performance of the organization.

Keep in mind that simultaneously improving True North measures takes significant change and will be a real challenge to achieve. It is a lot of hard work, especially for leadership levels. It is not a free lunch, but it can impact your numbers in a way that is hard to imagine—if you can drive the change and build the momentum of your people necessary to truly transform.

❑ Recordable accident rate		−81%
❑ Warranty costs		−69%
❑ Lead time	From 6 weeks to 5 days	
➢ Mixed truck load, build-to-dealer order		
❑ Complete and on time	From 84% to 98%	
❑ Enterprise productivity		+38%
❑ Inventory turnover		+171%
❑ Sales/square foot		+131%
❑ Operating income percent		+221%
❑ Return on assets		+237%
❑ Cash flow		+519%

HD, Q, D, and C drive all financial metrics

FIGURE 3.8
Manufactured fireplace firm after seven years of lean.

SUMMARY

I have yet to meet an executive who comes into a lean transformation thinking that it will be possible to increase his or her organization's productivity by fourfold, reduce quality errors by 99 percent, or reduce lead time by 95 percent. And yet those are the documented norms for a true enterprise transformation. Those few executives who do conceive that these levels of achievement might be possible must grasp that it will probably take a decade to accomplish. At the beginning, perhaps, this timeline is a discouraging thought. But the odd thing is, after you have made these kinds of annual improvements for a few years, you want to make sure it continues. So if, after the first few years of a lean transformation, you start to run out of improvement ideas to hit a particular target area, review all the lean tools (see the Foundations section) that principally impact that True North metric. Then, evaluate the breadth and depth of application of each of those tools. It *always* turns out that, by widening the spread of those core tools (and, if necessary, increasing the portion of kaizen events dedicated to that True North metric), additional improvement opportunities exist.

NOTES

1. Robert D. Buzzell and Bradley T. Gale, *The PIMS Principles: Linking Strategy to Performance* (New York: Free Press, 1987).
2. Source unknown.
3. George Stalk and Thomas Hout, *Competing Against Time: How Time-Based Competition Is Reshaping Global Markets* (New York: Free Press, 1990).
4. Paul D. Mango and Louis A. Shapiro, "Hospitals Get Serious About Operations," *McKinsey Quarterly*, no. 2 (May 2001): 74–85.

4

Value Stream Analysis Provides the Improvement Plan—And Kaizen Events Make It Happen

A *value stream* is the sequence of work steps that make value flow from customer request to customer fulfillment. In the case of a manufacturing firm, the value streams within a given operation are usually the key product families that are produced. Each family of product normally has somewhat different flows and key processes—and that is its value stream. At the start, there may be crossovers between value streams that disrupt the flow, but these are usually eliminated as the improvement effort progresses.

In a healthcare environment, for example, it is a sequence of services that make up the individual value stream. A patient diagnosed with AMI (acute myocardial infarction; a heart attack) will follow a specific series of work steps for further diagnosis and treatment, through discharge and billing. These steps form the value stream. In the case of the British Royal Navy, an aircraft carrier is a single (although complex) value stream; its output is sustainable sortie rate, that is, the ability to keep more planes in the air that can defend the fleet or attack enemy targets.

So a value stream is the path of work that flows a service or product to a customer. It is important to get the idea that it does not matter whether the value stream produces a product or a service, because the concepts still apply in roughly the same manner. To take the healthcare example, ThedaCare initially looked at the value stream within one of its main operations. The initial-state value stream analysis (VSA) is shown in Figure 4.1.

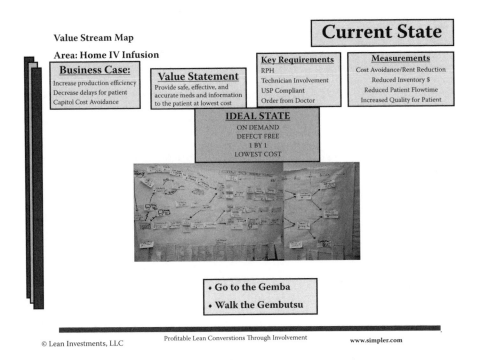

FIGURE 4.1
ThedaCare: Initial-state value stream map.

TAKING A WALK TO CREATE AN INITIAL-STATE VSA

The creation of the initial-state value stream is done, quite literally, by walking the value stream step by step. It is critically important to determine the actual work practices that are being followed day to day. This walk through the world of actual work is always eye-opening. It is never as the paper or computer says it is. There will be tasks you thought people were doing that they are not doing. And just as often, there will be tasks that they are doing as part of their daily work that you had no idea they were doing.

What you find is that no one in the entire organization can tell you all the steps in the current value stream. The individuals doing the work do not know what work others in the value stream are doing, so there is a lot of rework designed into today's processes. You may find that workers have been trained by talking to the outgoing worker or by his or her boss for a short period. The result is that they walk away with a list of work steps to do, without knowing why they should do these work steps. This approach leads to a lack of knowledge sufficient to even provide a basis for improving the process.

Furthermore, in the case of administrative processes, we tend to swoop in when there is a problem, redesign a few steps, almost always adding some extra inspection or rework steps, and then depart (after all, there are other fires to fight, so we could not spend the time to actually understand this process from end to end). The net effect is that the typical administrative process has a negative productivity growth rate of 1 percent to 2 percent per year from the firefighting approach to improvement.

Initial-State VSA and the True North Metrics

The initial-state VSA does a couple of things. The analysis provides the base level for the process. A good initial state should, at a minimum, document the value streams performance against the four True North metrics. So there should be some human development measures taken during the analysis—things like accident rates, turnover rates, and so on. There should also be quality data gathered, and the data should show where the key issues are (the raw material for a quality Pareto chart). The initial-state analysis should also show where delays occur and where the flow is blocked. And, of course, the analysis should show where human resources are consumed.

Most materials on value stream analysis have missed the True North metrics aspect. Instead, they typically have focused on people/productivity measures and time/delivery measures, but have missed the quality and human development metrics. A baseline is needed for all four True North measures.

Helping You See the Waste

An initial-state VSA is usually the first step in learning to see waste. For this reason, I strongly recommend that the leadership team of the business unit should be the team to conduct the first value stream analysis in the startup of a lean transformation. As this team determines the status of each work step—is this value-added or is it non-value-added, that is, if customers saw us doing this step would they want to pay for it. This will be the first time the leadership gets a personal picture of what waste actually looks like in a value stream that they own.

Seeing this waste does two things: (1) it begins the leadership on a path to learning what waste looks like, and (2) it begins to provide leadership with the motivation to improve. When you document real work, it is pretty hard to come away thinking that what you've just seen is a fine-tuned value stream that cannot be improved. In the early stages of lean, learning to see waste by the senior leadership is by far the most important impact of a good value stream analysis.

In the diagram itself, each key waste is usually noted with a waste opportunity *burst* (callout). A little graphic that notes an area of the value stream where improvement is needed and the type of improvement needed. These bursts inform the next steps, in which you apply the various lean improvement tools.

Without getting into a detailed discussion of each of the tools in the lean tool kit, suffice it to note that there are tools that address key issues with each True North metric area. If there is flow blockage and time being consumed, you may, for instance, use set-up reduction to reduce batch sizes. You may set up a kanban to minimize flow disruption around a monument process (a single process that constricts the flow of multiple value streams through a single process step). You may establish one-piece flow to keep the process moving, and so on. There are lean principles and tools that primarily address issues in each True North metric area (see Figure 4.2).

Improvement Dimension

Human Development	Quality	Delivery / Flow	Cost / Productivity
Team Participation	Zero Defects	Takt Time	N.V.A. /V.A.
6S	5 Whys	One Piece Flow	Standard Work
Safe Workplace Design	Andon	Pull	Shojinka
Ergonomic Kaizen	Poka –Yoke	Load Load	
Teian Suggestion System	Self / Successive Checks	S.M.E.D.	
	7 Statistical Tools	Kanban	
	CEDAC	T.P.M.	
	FMEA	3P	
	Taguchi Methods	Supply Chain Development	
		Heijunka	

TVSA
TPOC
Strategy Deployment
Lean Practices

FIGURE 4.2
The four True North metrics.

BRAINSTORMING TO CREATE AN IDEAL-STATE VALUE STREAM

After documenting the initial state of the value stream, the team then brainstorms about the ideal value stream. The idea is to try to envision what this value stream could look like if all the non-value-added steps could be removed. It will not actually be possible to remove all the non-value-added steps in the first improvement pass through the value stream, but by taking a look at this "perfect process," you set the improvement bar high. Normally, when you work on improving an area, you think about improving it by some meaningful (but small) amount, say, a 5 percent improvement. You would see this result as a significant step ahead.

One key aspect of determining the ideal state is to see what a flow process could really look like. This flow process will typically have something like 95 percent fewer steps than the current process. So if you start with this "ideal" value stream as your point of reference and think in terms of adding back as few steps as possible, the ideal provides you with a different paradigm for your improvement, as shown in Figure 4.3. This paradigm will typically involve removing about half of the total steps in the value stream. This view of the value stream will lead you to set improvement goals for removing half the steps, instead only of 5 percent of the steps. This will be an order of magnitude improvement from the usual practice.

CREATING A FUTURE-STATE VALUE STREAM

The next step is to create a future-state value stream that represents the improvement you actually plan to do in this value stream over the next six to eighteen months (see Figure 4.4).

In this step, you identify the key waste opportunity bursts and set up a work plan to address each of them. This work plan is usually made up of three kinds of effort. Some of the improvements will be *just-do-its*, quick-hit fixes that become obvious as you conduct the value stream analysis and can be assigned to an individual to implement immediately. Other (very few) improvements will involve a traditional project-type of effort. An example might be a change in software to fit with the new

Value Stream Maps

Area: Home IV Infusion

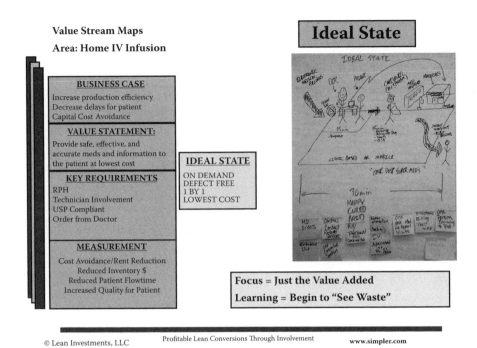

BUSINESS CASE

Increase production efficiency
Decrease delays for patient
Capital Cost Avoidance

VALUE STATEMENT:

Provide safe, effective, and
accurate meds and information to
the patient at lowest cost

KEY REQUIREMENTS

RPH
Technician Involvement
USP Compliant
Order from Doctor

MEASUREMENT

Cost Avoidance/Rent Reduction
Reduced Inventory $
Reduced Patient Flowtime
Increased Quality for Patient

Ideal State

IDEAL STATE

ON DEMAND
DEFECT FREE
1 BY 1
LOWEST COST

Focus = Just the Value Added

Learning = Begin to "See Waste"

© Lean Investments, LLC   Profitable Lean Conversions Through Involvement   www.simpler.com

FIGURE 4.3
ThedaCare: Ideal-state map.

work practices. But the major improvement impact will come from kaizen events focused on making substantial and fast improvements within the value stream in just one week.

Improvement Goals

A key aspect of this future-state value stream is to set improvement goals for each True North metric (see Figure 4.5).

At the beginning, you will not know how high you should set your improvement goals. If you were able to see lots and lots of value streams done in many kinds of organizations, what you would find is that, as a rough average, you should think in terms of *halving*. You should target cutting out half of the total work steps in the process by the time you implement all the events, projects, and do-its. So if you cut the work steps in half, it is reasonable to think you can reduce needed human resource in this value

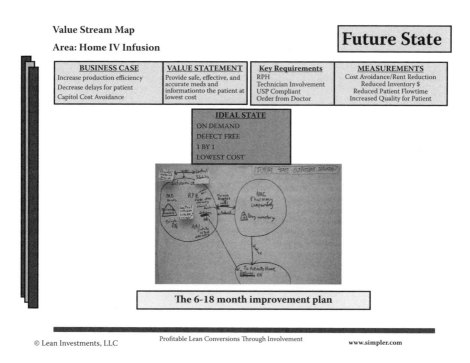

Value Stream Map

Area: Home IV Infusion

Future State

BUSINESS CASE	VALUE STATEMENT	Key Requirements	MEASUREMENTS
Increase production efficiency	Provide safe, effective, and	RPH	Cost Avoidance/Rent Reduction
Decrease delays for patient	accurate meds and	Technician Involvement	Reduced Inventory $
Capitol Cost Avoidance	informationto the patient at	USP Compliant	Reduced Patient Flowtime
	lowest cost	Order from Doctor	Increased Quality for Patient

IDEAL STATE

ON DEMAND

DEFECT FREE

1 BY 1

LOWEST COST

The 6-18 month improvement plan

© Lean Investments, LLC — Profitable Lean Conversions Through Involvement — www.simpler.com

FIGURE 4.4

ThedaCare: Future-state value stream map.

stream by half, reduce errors/defects by half, and expect to reduce flow times/lead times by half. If this were the first time you were to do a value stream analysis, you would probably balk at setting improvement targets this high. Yet if you do not set high goals, you certainly will not achieve high levels of performance. This halving, then, is a good place to start, because it is significant, yet it is pretty normal in terms of lean results. If you still find these high levels of improvement difficult to embrace, you may need a sensei who has lived through this kind of improvement to push you and your organization to set goals that are appropriate for a solid value stream improvement effort. My Toyota sensei normally summarized good targets for a value stream improvement plan with the phrase "halve the bad and double the good"

One of the key deliverables during a future-state value stream mapping event is to be sure that you have a solid, achievable implementation plan (see Figure 4.6).

R.I. EVENT REPORT

Location: ThedaCare   Date: 1/18/05

RESULTS:

1:

Team Topic	Measurements of Results	Before	Future Potential	% Change	Comments
Home IV Infusion VSA	Patient Flowtime (hrs)	4.0	2.5	−38%	
	Sum Manual Touch Times	6.7	4.5	−33%	
	Inventory $ @ THAC	$75,657	$25,000	−67%	
	Inventory Turns @ THAC	13.9	24.0	−73%	Duplicate Inventory
	Miles Driven Fox Point to AMC / Yr	15,600	5,200	−67%	
	Handoffs Outpatient	6.0	3.0	−50%	
	Handoffs Home Care	9.0	4.0	−56%	
	Annual Rent Required	$ 56,000	$ -	−100%	Required to maintain 2 Pharm Labs
	Required Capital to Renovate Pharm Lab @ Fox Point	$ 200,000	$ -	−100%	Will consolidate into AMC

surveys			
1 (overall satisfaction):	4.1	5 (initial presentation):	4.0
2 (consultant perf.):	4.6	6 (participate in future):	4.4
3 (results impact):	4.3	7 (leaders' meetings):	
4 (learning experience)	4.4	8 (prod'n sys. principles):	4.1
Key Manager Survey Score/10:	8.9	comments:	Rick Berry: TCAH Manager ... GREAT JOB!

9 (prep. and team): 4.0
10 (reason for topics): 4.6
Overall Avg. (Q1 to Q10): 4.3
Comments +: 9 -: 3

Profitable Lean Conversions Through Involvement

© Lean Investments, LLC   www.simpler.com

FIGURE 4.5
ThedaCare: Results.

Action Plan

ThedaCare at Home: IV Infusion VSA

Impact Key: $ = Reduced Cost   Q = Increased Quality   CS = Increased Customer Satisfaction   EOC = Increased Employer of Choice

Event	Project	Do It	Description	Who	Impact	Date*	Comments	Status
					Plan		**Deliverables**	
X			Infusion Intake & Clinical Evaluation Process (17, 46, 3, 15, 24)		$Q CS EOC			
X			Centralized Compounding Standard Work @ AMC (36, 24, 22, 11)		$		Improvements at AMC Pharm to prepare for move from Fox Point	
X			Centralized Compounding 6S Event @ AMC (10, 2, 34)		$		Improvements at AMC Pharm to prepare for move from Fox Point	
X			Create Outpatient Infusion Cell @ AMC (21, 28, 44)		$Q CS EOC			
X			Inventory Consolidation / Kanban (19, 38)		$ EOC			
	X		Standardize clinical role of outpatient infusion for RNs (13, 9, 35, 43, 18)		Q EOC			
	X		Improve process for delivery to home		$			
	X		Computer System Integration (30, 8, 14)		$Q CS EOC			
		X	Transfer of Services to DME (5)		$			
		X	Insurance Database (36)		$ CS			

© Lean Investments, LLC   Profitable Lean Conversions Through Involvement   www.simpler.com

FIGURE 4.6
ThedaCare: Action plan.

Work Plan and Responsibilities

The future-state work plan should set out dates and responsibilities for each do-it, each project, and each kaizen event. Doing a value stream analysis without developing an improvement work plan or implementing actual improvement is *muda*—or waste in itself! You will occasionally find organizations that have done lots of value stream documentation, but never get around to actually improving anything—that's muda.

A final caution on constructing value streams: Computerizing your value streams seems to be a common disease that has spread throughout most organizations. You should vaccinate your organization against this disease. A computerized map is stored on—well, a computer—which makes it pretty inaccessible and difficult to be seen in a simultaneous mode by a team of people. It is far better to have your value stream displayed in a very visual manner in a very public area near the *gemba* (workplace). This forces a deeper level of learning and creates a visual and team-based approach. In addition, only someone with strong computer skills will be able to draw a computerized value stream, and you want anyone to be able to draw one.

In the Post-It Note kind of value stream depiction, everyone can participate in the construction and modification of the value stream. If the people who do the work and who supervise the work aren't involved in the development of and modifications to the value stream map, the whole change-management effort may stall.

THE RULE OF 5X

Many senior managers use an interesting paradigm when approaching improvements: Do it perfectly the first time *and* get the full result of the approach. This is sort of a big bang view of improvement. With lean, however, there is an understanding that you cannot see all the waste when you first look at a value stream. After you have conducted your first complete cycle of value stream improvement—say, after eighteen months of hard work, studying every work step in your value stream and making the key improvements outlined in the initial work plan—then it is time to start again.

What you will find is that the first pass of value stream improvement did, in fact, result in significant improvement. But something else very interesting happened. Those improvements also made the next level of waste visible. So, if you start all over and redocument your newly improved value stream step by step, you will be able to come up with a second pass. A new value stream improvement plan that will typically take out half of the remaining steps—and defects—and time in the value stream.

Becoming lean is all about doing this many times, not once. A good rule of thumb is to think in terms of planning to study every value stream, every work process at least five times (or "5X") before you think you are becoming lean. If you realize that you need to plan to do this level of process study, you will think very differently about how you organize to support your lean transformation.

Every restudy takes you to a new level of performance and is profitable by itself. After you have gone through every value stream five times, you will typically have removed about 90 percent of the waste that you started with, and you will have reduced errors and defects by 90 percent, reduced time to provide the product or service by 90 percent, reduced the needed labor by 80 percent (yes, 80 percent!), and reduced accident rates and member turnover rates by 90 percent. These numbers are hard to believe, but those few organizations that have actually gone through value streams five or more times have achieved these levels of improvement. But the most important achievement is that your organization will have taught yourselves to believe in *continuous* improvement. Very few organizations manage to get this idea. I think that very few people really comprehend the phrase "continuous improvement." People may hear the words, but what they think is "step improvement"; in other words, "I am going to do this thing, get this gain, and then be done."

Organizations that have done five passes (5X) of improvement through their value streams do not need to push improvement. By that time, everyone in the organization knows that, as Henry Ford said, "Our own attitude is that we are chartered with discovering the best way of doing everything, and that we must regard every process employed in the business today as purely experimental."[1]

As an example, the HMMWV (Humvee) value stream at the U.S. Army's Red River Army Depot (RRAD) had problems accelerating the up-armoring of HMMWVs to protect soldiers from improvised explosive devices (IEDs). If you initially saw this issue in the news, you may also recall that it disappeared from the news about a year later. The reason was the accelerated rate of lean implementation in the remanufacturing and up-armoring process within the U.S. Army Materiel Command.

Figure 4.7 shows the expansion of output at the Red River Amy Depot over a fourteen-month period of time, within the same floor space, with a threefold increase in productivity. The team at Red River was able to achieve over a 200-fold increase in output per week. Of course, this did not happen with one easy pass through the value stream. As Figure 4.7 shows, the first pass HMMWV value stream took only about four months but also achieved a 20-fold improvement in output. Much more was needed. So the folks at Red River started all over again. They redid their value stream analysis based on the new and improved value stream that came from a detailed gemba walk. They came up with many more waste opportunity bursts and proceeded to attack these with kaizen events, do-its, and projects. After about eight months, they achieved roughly a 140-fold improvement, but still more was needed. So they again walked the newly improved value stream looking for opportunities for improvement, and then started implementing a new value stream improvement plan. This third pass took them to just over a 200-fold improvement in output per week. Within a few months, they achieved their required output rate. Thus, with three consecutive passes through this value stream, they were able to make a

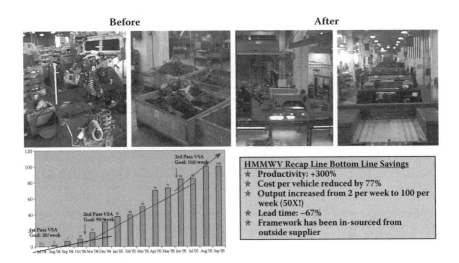

FIGURE 4.7
Red River Army Depot: HMMWV lean transformation.

dramatic increase in output and productivity, and also provide dramatically increased protection for U.S. troops in Iraq.

As another example of multiple passes through a value stream, recall our review of Watlow's use of this idea to improve its customer-facing processes in its custom heater business (see Chapter 3). In very round numbers, the industry norm was to take about three months (three one-month customer processes consisting of quoting, engineering, and prototype building) to complete the bidding process, at which point they earn about 15 percent of the bids as orders. Watlow's business was growing about 3 percent per year. We knew that when we started lean in the production areas that we would free up production resources at something like a 20 percent per year rate. So, instead of starting the lean work in production, we decided to start with the three one-month customer processes (see Figure 4.8).

The impact was almost immediate. By the time Watlow was in the midst of the second pass through each of these value streams, its growth rate had surpassed the fourfold expectation—and now it really was time to get going in production areas!

An interesting sidelight of this work was the administrative productivity aspect. What you find is that working the four True North metric areas creates a synergistic effect on total results. So in addition to the productivity growth that came from dropping non-value-added steps in the quote–engineer–prototype build processes, the over fourfold increase in win rates amounted to a greater than fourfold productivity gain due to the impact of fast response on win rates—and that is in addition to the productivity from dropping non-value-added steps to get to the faster cycles.

One other corporate example of making multiple passes on the same value stream comes from one of the Shingo Prize–winning operations: the Freudenberg-NOK GP (FNOK) business in Ligonier, Indiana. Ligonier produces a variety of vibration-control products used in all kinds of automotive applications (this was also the plant where Simpler Consulting sensei Terry Rousch, who helped edit this book, was the TVD lead center general supervisor).

What you see in Figure 4.9 is the impact of multiple passes through the same value stream. This is the "relentless pursuit of perfection," as the phrase goes. The starting point productivity was 55 pieces per associate per hour. In its first weeklong kaizen event in the work area, team members increased the output to 86 pieces per hour. This was about a 50 percent

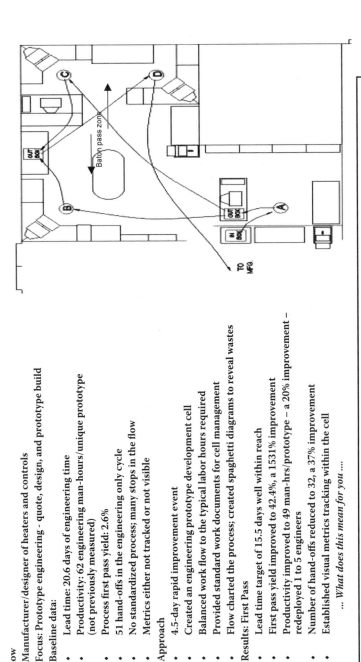

□ Watlow

Manufacturer/designer of heaters and controls

Focus: Prototype engineering - quote, design, and prototype build

Baseline data:

- Lead time: 20.6 days of engineering time
- Productivity: 62 engineering man-hours/unique prototype (not previously measured)
- Process first pass yield: 2.6%
- 51 hand-offs in the engineering only cycle
- No standardized process; many stops in the flow
- Metrics either not tracked or not visible

Approach

- 4.5-day rapid improvement event
- Created an engineering prototype development cell
- Balanced work flow to the typical labor hours required
- Provided standard work documents for cell management
- Flow charted the process; created spaghetti diagrams to reveal wastes

Results: First Pass

- Lead time target of 15.5 days well within reach
- First pass yield improved to 42.4%, a 1531% improvement
- Productivity improved to 49 man-hrs/prototype – a 20% improvement – redeployed 1 to 5 engineers
- Number of hand-offs reduced to 32, a 37% improvement
- Established visual metrics tracking within the cell

... *What does this mean for you ....*

Goal = Implement three passes of this value stream = Provide quotes, designs, and prototypes in one-quarter the time = Grow 2 to 4 times the industry standard

FIGURE 4.8

Engineering: Quote design and prototype.

Repeat Kaizens on the Same Part Number

FNGP Ligonier, Indiana, Factory, 1992–1994

	FEB 1992	APRIL 1992	MAY 1992	NOV 1992	JAN 1993	JAN 1994	AUG 1995
Number of associates	21	18	15	12	6	3	3
Pieces made per associate	55	86	112	140	225	450	600
Spaces utilized (sq. ft.)	2,300	2,000	1,850	1,662	1,360	1,200	1,200

•At least six complete reviews of each process are necessary to achieve full lean results

•Given good preparation and follow up, more Kaizen event = more results

Baseline performance before start of lean initiative on this three-shift operation with seven associates per shift.
During this period, OSHA reportable accidents and workers' compensation costs both declined by more than 92%. Total capital spending over this period was less than $1,000 for a right-sized, in-line painting system permitting single-piece flow.   Source: *Lean Thinking*, Womack & Jones

FIGURE 4.9
Reversal of law of diminishing returns.

productivity increase. Many organizations would have thought "wow, we have increased productivity 50 percent—I guess we must have gotten all the improvement we can," and then have left the area for good!

FNOK went back to the same area the next month and restudied the area again and got an additional 30 percent productivity gain. It then went back six months later and did it again; this time it got a 20-plus percent gain. Given the law of diminishing returns, if you had the fortitude to stick with this for three passes, you would begin to think that the gains were getting smaller and it was probably time to go improve someplace else. However, the FNOK team stuck to it and went back again two months later and got a 60 percent productivity gain. Again, not satisfied, they came back a year later and were able to get a 100 percent productivity gain, to 450 pieces per hour. And then eight months later FNOK hit it again, with a 30 percent productivity gain. The end result at that point was that its output per person was more than ten times the starting point (proving that it is possible to reduce work content by 90 percent if you are willing to aggressively restudy an area several times). Realistically, most of us would have stopped at the first 50 percent. And that is the difference between most of us and those few who actually relentlessly pursue perfection.

At the time of the Ligonier Shingo Prize Award, FNOK had been, as a corporation, on the lean journey for six years. In that time, the company had conducted more than 8,000 weeklong kaizen improvement events, resulting in a corporate-wide quality improvement from more than 2,000 ppm to less than 50 ppm, reduction of work in process inventory of more than 80 percent, while generating a corporate-wide productivity gain of over 175 percent. That's the power of lean, applied *continuously*.

A MODEL VALUE STREAM

ThedaCare's first several years of improving hospital value streams led it to go back and take it from scratch in the fourth year of its lean journey. ThedaCare decided to attempt to create the model for the future of healthcare. This is what Toyota would refer to as a *model line*. The purpose of the model line is to create an example that is so advanced in its overall performance that anyone observing it can easily see that this is a successful approach exhibiting a breakthrough level of performance. A model line is both a highly developed example and a key change-management tool.

The model line is normally the first area that goes through the multiple passes of improvement. The multiple passes create breakthrough results, but the area also begins to operate in new ways and begins to develop lean management practices. The model line both demonstrates the power of lean and begins to build a new learning culture that will sustain the improvements for the long term. It is the model for the future of the rest of the organization—in results, in developing people, and in building a new culture of continuous improvement. To create its model line, then ThedaCare CEO John Toussaint (John is now CEO of the Thedacare Center for Healthcare Value—an institution aiming to improve value in the whole healthcare system) looked at the core healthcare delivery value streams in ThedaCare's flagship hospital by using value stream analysis and set up a major new work plan for the next level of improvement (see Figure 4.10).

In this redesign of its core value streams, ThedaCare redesigned the work processes of physicians, pharmacists, and nurses, and also redesigned the physical structure of the hospital floors to fit a new model of flow and collaborative care. In the collaborative care model line, the patient is cared for by a team made up of the nurse, physician, and pharmacist. The team is there at the start to set the plan of care for that patient in a team-based

Reinvention of a Core Healthcare Value Stream

❏ A vision of hospital care with nursing at its center
❏ A new model of inpatient care delivery based on:
  ➢ Change in team roles and responsibilities (<u>people</u>)
  ➢ Innovation (<u>processes</u>)
  ➢ Principles of poka-yoke, pull production, and visual management
❏ Provided in an environment designed specifically for the model, to reduce waste, to ensure safety, and to promote healing.
❏ Enabled by T.I.S.
  ➢ Three vertical value streams
  ➢ Twenty-eight RIEs/projects

FIGURE 4.10
ThedaCare: Collaborative care.

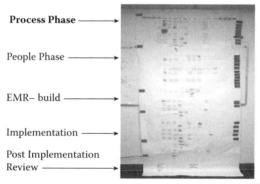

Process Phase
People Phase
EMR– build
Implementation
Post Implementation Review

THEDA♥CARE

FIGURE 4.11
Planning: Vertical value stream map.

approach, using the combined knowledge and experience of all three disciplines.

The process of creating this model value stream actually was based on the development of three vertical value streams and twenty-eight kaizen events. (*Note:* The vertical value stream map is a tool developed by Simpler Consulting for lean project management, as shown in Figure 4.11.)

ThedaCare's model line demonstrates the application of a number of key lean concepts, including *poka-yoke* (mistake proofing) and *jidoka* (stopping the process to fix errors). In addition, ThedaCare incorporated the true voice of the customer by inviting ThedaCare patients to be members

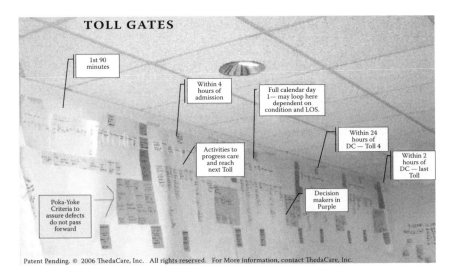

FIGURE 4.12
Value stream toll gates.

of the improvement team. Figure 4.12 shows where toll gates were built in to the process flow to assure quality of patient care.

Overall, the ThedaCare model line reduced error rates by more than 80 percent at an organization that was already a national benchmark for patient quality performance. In addition, by flowing care to patients, the average length of stay was reduced by 28 percent, despite a slight increase in severity rates. The financial impact was a cost reduction in per-patient stay of more than 30 percent. This was truly a breakthrough level of health-care performance.

THE POWER OF WEEKLONG KAIZEN EVENTS

The dramatic improvement examples noted at ThedaCare, the Red River Army Depot, FNOK, and the British Royal Navy were all built with the use of weeklong kaizen events. Toyota has used the weeklong kaizen event since its early days. In Toyota speak, it is called a *jishukin* (voluntary study) event. In daily use, it was often referred to as a "five day and one night" event because of the intensity of the work effort expected of the team members—the concept being that you worked so hard on improvement in that week, that you only got the equivalent of one night's sleep. This idea reminds me of Marine Corps boot camp practice; part of the initial approach of weeklong kaizen events was for the same reason that the Marine Corp does it—to push you so hard they break you down and then rebuild you in the new model.

There were many experiments in the Ohno days about the ideal structure for these kaizen events. In the end, the weeklong structure proved to be best. It was long enough that you could take a significant chunk of a value stream and both redesign it and *implement* the new process during the same week. It was also short enough that you could not take a long time discussing whether you were going to do it or not if you were going to finish by week's end. Much of the early kaizen event design was based on principles of change management—the realization that to drive improvement, they would first need to get folks to go to the gemba (the workplace) and actually make changes to the work and not just study the work.

So there was an intensity that you rarely see today. When my Japanese sensei first started teaching me, we were close to the original model. Although this was very exciting, over time, we decided that we could achieve the needed impact with a bit less stress and a bit more sleep!

Kaizen events are the primary mechanism for instituting improvement to value streams. One reason is that we are typically organized around the model of firefighting in the way we run our daily businesses. In this model, the adrenalin rush of the firefighting *always* pushes out the steady focus needed for root-cause improvement. Although daily improvement is the long-term objective, it is more of a long-term end state than a way to get there. If you focus on daily improvement in a firefighting organization, the firefighting will always win, and you will find that you are not spending any time on root-cause process improvement. So one benefit of kaizen events is that, as a business leader, you know that you have a half dozen of your team members focused on improving things for at least that week. If you run your kaizen events well and follow up thoroughly (which for most firms is *not* the case in the first year or so), your rate of improvement is pretty much proportional to the pace of kaizen events. Again, a key assumption being that you run the events well and you are diligent in the follow-up in the areas studied (of course, this is normally not the case, a side effect of the firefighting style that we usually start with).

Another aspect of weeklong kaizen events is that they are learning experiences for the team members. As a *Fortune* magazine article on Toyota noted, "Toyota has long maintained that the Toyota Way can only be grasped through constant practice in the workplace under the tutelage of a deeply experienced master."[2] Kaizen teams are ideally coached by someone with deep experience in the application of the lean tools, practices, principles, and lean leadership behaviors.

From my personal observations at Danaher and HON/HNI, it became apparent that you could count the number of weeklong kaizen event experiences as you would college-degree credit hours. In terms of getting a college-degree level of lean knowledge, you can count each event week that you *personally* participate in full time as a credit hour. Typically about a dozen weeks of this intense application experience is roughly like graduating from kindergarten. You know that it works, but are pretty unsure about what to do to replicate your success in another area. If you keep on the learning curve and keep accumulating kaizen event experiences, you find another threshold at about thirty-six to forty events; at this point you are familiar with most of the lean tools that are being used inside your business and are competent as a team member to use them. The interesting thing is that although you know how to use the tools, you typically do not yet believe in the core lean principles and consequently will often go awry in application of the tools. You do not yet really believe in the principles that you are supposed to apply when using the tools, so you can often get off track because the principles will feel wrong for a very long time (the core lean principles are easy to understand, but they are the exact opposite of how we have been taught to organize work, so they are very hard to apply). It turns out that if you follow your sensei's lead and continue to build event experiences, somewhere around sixty events, you begin to believe the principles, and you are now able to lead kaizen efforts effectively because you not only know the tools, but also implement them in a way that's consistent with the principles of lean.

Somewhere around 100 event experiences, you find that individuals undergo a personal transformation—the word *conversion* also comes to mind. These folks have seen that applying the tools and following the principles have always led to significant improvement, regardless of the kind of work being studied, and they now know what is possible. This makes them frustrated with the current state of waste, and, very importantly, self-motivated to drive improvement—forever! At this point, you find that individuals will drive forward with lean improvement regardless of the support they get. In fact, they will change organizations, if necessary, to keep working in an environment where improvement is the norm. These individuals are now ready to be sensei in their own right.

When you have developed a cadre of these folks who have significant personal experience, you are on the road to self-sustaining continuous improvement. The key is not that they know everything there is to know about lean, but that they are now absolutely sure that they know how to create improvement and that they will never stop.

Weeklong kaizen events are how you get lean results, but they are also how you learn, and, further on, they are also how you become motivated to improve forever, so they have a cultural impact. The right way to think about kaizen events is that they provide three kinds of results: improved business results, basic learning in tools/principles and practices, and a cultural change that builds a true learning organization that will drive improvement forever. It becomes a bit like the mountain climber's explanation for why he climbs a mountain: "Because it is there." The lean leader's attitude to waste is the same: "I work to remove waste because it is there."

For an organization, kaizen events can be used as a measure of culture change or attitude change. The end result is that weeklong lean kaizen event participation creates new attitudes and behaviors. When I joined HON, I required every general manager to get a dozen kaizen events under his or her belt during the first year—they all had to graduate from kindergarten. One of these business unit general managers, Dave Melhus (now chief administrative officer at Simpler), went on to be the executive vice president for Vermeer manufacturing. He started the lean effort there. He had gone through the kindergarten training program and knew that it had an impact. So Dave and Mary Andringa, CEOs of Vermeer, did an analysis after about two years of lean effort at Vermeer. They compared the scores on its member survey to the number of lean events that each individual had been on (see Figure 4.13).

The numbers in Figure 4.13 are the variation from the company's average score for that particular member survey question (the typical score was in the 50s). So, for instance, if you had not been on any kaizen events, your attitude toward your supervisor was slightly negative compared to the company-wide average, a rating of −3. If you had been on one or two kaizen events, you moved to slightly positive in terms of your attitude toward your supervisor, a +3. If you had been on three to five kaizen events, you

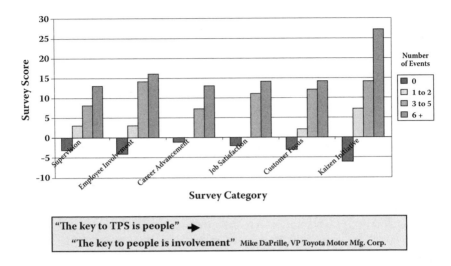

FIGURE 4.13
Survey scores compared to event participation.

moved to a +8 score on attitude toward your supervisor, and if you had been on six or more events, you moved to a +13. With typical average scores for most of these questions, a +13 was a really big difference.

Going through the key questions in the member survey, it was evident that the more kaizen event experience you had, the better you felt about the company: you liked your supervisor, you felt good about employee involvement and career advancement opportunities, you had higher job satisfaction, and you became more customer focused. Altogether, you had fundamentally improved your outlook on your workplace. This is a measure of the culture-building impact of the weeklong lean event experience.

A similar study at ThedaCare of the impact on attitudes/culture change of event participation is shown in Figure 4.14. In this particular instance, seven of the ten areas surveyed showed that the satisfaction scores moved in a positive direction. Of those who participated in two or more events, the overall satisfaction level was higher and the key emphasis category identified was "I would recommend this organization to a friend as a good place to work." The other major finding of this study was that the positive increase in attitudes toward the organization increased rapidly and significantly from the second event through the eighth event. After eight events, the survey scores began to level off at an exceptionally high level of personal commitment to the organization.

Questions	Count	Mean	Mean	Strongly Disagree	Agree	Disagree	Strongly Disagree
13. I would recommend this organization to a friend as a good place to work.	306	3.39		42.8%	53.6%	2.9%	0.7%
14. Overall, I think this is a great place to work.	315	3.37		41.6%	54.9%	2.9%	0.6%
10. My manager or someone at work seems to care about me as a person.	318	3.34		38.4%	57.5%	3.5%	0.6%
6. My manager shows appreciation for the work I do.	318	3.23		33.3%	58.8%	5.7%	2.2%
5. At work, my opinions seem to count.	319	3.21		31.7%	58.9%	8.5%	0.9%
11. People here are willing to give extra to get the job done.	316	3.19		31.0%	58.2%	9.5%	1.3%
7. My manager provides me with sufficient opportunities to improve myself.	315	3.16		28.6%	60.3%	9.5%	1.6%
12. I am satisfied with my job security.	313	3.15		27.5%	62.0%	8.9%	1.6%
8. People are encouraged to balance their work and personal life.	317	2.98		17.4%	64.7%	16.4%	1.6%
9. Management has kept promises made to us.	311	2.89		12.5%	66.2%	19.3%	1.9%
Overall Averages	314.8	3.19		30.5%	59.5%	8.7%	1.3%

> ❑ Statistically significant differences (improvement in satisfaction) on 7 of the 10 items for those involved in RIEs)
> ❑ Satisfaction increases rapidly until reaching a plateau at about eight experiences
> ❑ Satisfaction is higher in employees who participate in two or more events
> ❑ The item with the greatest satisfaction is "I would recommend this organization to friend as a good place to work"

FIGURE 4.14

RIE (event) participation survey.

SUMMARY

Value stream analysis is a way to provide a plan and a way to begin to learn how to see waste. And the more times you go through a given value stream, the better it becomes; so one of your early objectives should be to select one value stream that you will go back to multiple times to prove to your organization that you really can improve continuously. In addition, kaizen events not only generate the lean gains you seek, but also provide the path for organizations to learn the tools, come to believe the principles, and begin to transform their cultures.

NOTES

1. Henry Ford and Samuel Crowther, *Today and Tomorrow* (Garden City, NY: Doubleday, Page & Company, 1926).
2. Clay Chandler, "Full Speed Ahead," *Fortune*, February 7, 2005.

5

Tactical Organizational Practices

In this chapter, I give an overview of a number of the day-to-day implementation practices of a lean transformation. I call these "tactical organizational practices" (as opposed to the higher-level, strategic organizational practices in Chapter 6), which include the link between double-digit annual improvement rates in the True North metrics and the pace of process study/improvement. I also look at some guidelines surrounding the level and type of support resources that make this pace something that can be sustained for the long term. I also look at some guidelines that are specific to supporting continuous improvement in administrative areas, as well as redeployment guidelines and practices. Essentially, this chapter gives you key lean practices that are essential to achieving lean results, while building organizational buy-in and morale. I tried several approaches before settling on the guidelines I discuss here. These may not be optimal practices, but they are workable ones that have succeeded consistently.

THE *n*/10 RULE

Your pace of overall improvement is roughly proportional to the pace of successful process study and change—in other words, to the pace of events that you implement in support of your value stream improvement plans. In fact, you can, very roughly, tie kaizen event pace to achievement of double-digit improvement gains in the four True North metrics (see Chapter 3). At the very least, there is a normal pace of events/process improvement that is required to deliver a given level of improvement results.

From experience at both Danaher and HON/HNI, a good long-term event pace of roughly $n/10$ seems to work well. The n is the number of people in the value stream being worked on (or in the total site under transformation or in the total company, if an enterprise-wide transformation is under way). Dividing the population by 10 ($n/10$ rule) gives the approximate number of annual events (that is, weeklong teams of six to eight people, studying and improving a process within a value stream). So in a site of 1,000 people, a long-term sustainable rate of process improvement would be about 100 kaizen events per year. This is a pace that should deliver double-digit gains in the four True North metrics, something in the range of 10 to 30 percent annual improvement in quality (external customer complaint rates, internal defect rates, etc.), lead time (customer lead times, inventory levels, etc.), cost (productivity at the enterprise level), and human development metrics (event participation rates, accident rates, turnover rates, etc.).

At the HON Company's seventeen business units, we targeted and met improvement rates that included:

- 20 percent annual accident rate reduction
- 20 percent annual reduction in both customer complaints and defect rates
- 50 percent annual reduction in lead times until we got to a single-day cycle (this was a principal strategic objective to assure higher growth from customer responsiveness, as a means of generating growth through lean, to absorb freed up resources—especially people resources—from the lean effort)
- 15 percent enterprise productivity growth (typically about 15 percent sales growth with the same employment levels each year)

These improvement rates are aggressive, but have been exceeded during other lean transformations I have witnessed. They take a lot of discipline, but a key point here is that you cannot expect these rates of improvement without doing the hard work of studying and improving processes—the $n/10$ rule part. Improving these four True North metrics at double-digit rates each year will drive every line item on the income statement and the balance sheet in the good direction. At HON, we basically grew 15 percent per year without adding new human resource (some normal attrition allowed for some new blood every year), without adding floor space (increased flow provided almost all the needed floor space), without add-ing much working capital (faster flow means less inventory per dollar of sales), and with reduced fixed capital per revenue dollar due to better uti-lization of capital assets.

To give you another example of how this works, take a look at the progress at Freudenburg-NOK (FNOK) during its lean transforma-tion, as outlined by its CEO, Joe Day, during a Shingo Prize Annual Convention. Figure 5.1 shows FNOK's annual event pace and annual net financial savings.

FNOK was roughly a 5,000 person organization, which targeted a more aggressive event pace of around $n/5$. At the $n/5$ pace, this resulted in a tar-get of 1,000 events per year. As FNOK started its journey, company leaders ramped up their effort over the first three years. The first year was 1992, which was a partial year due to midyear startup, and employees conducted 200 events in various business units that year, generating $2 million dol-lars of net savings. In 1993 (the first full year), they ran 600 events and had net savings of $4 million. In 1994, they hit their target event pace of 1,000 events per year, which they then held for the next seven years. The interest-ing thing is that the annual savings ran $7 million per year in 1994, 1995, and 1996. By 1997, as their skills matured and as they began to have true sensei grow internally, FNOK's net savings grew to $16 million. The fol-lowing year, 1998, with additional maturity, FNOK saved $19 million. In 1999, savings grew to $21 million, then grew again in 2000 to $30 million,

Freudenburg NOK (FNOK) Corporate-Wide

	1992	1993	1994	1995	1996	1997	1998	1999	2000	2001
# of Events	200	600	1000	1000	1000	1000	1000	1000	1000	1000
$ Savings in millions	2	4	7	7	7	16	19	21	30	31

> **IF YOU CONTINUE APPLYING THE TOOLS, YOU CONTINUE TO GENERATE SAVINGS**

FIGURE 5.1
Reversal of law of diminishing returns.

and again in 2001 (the year prior to the Shingo talk) to $31 million. This is one of those counterintuitive aspects of lean; normally we would expect diminishing returns over time with continued application of the same tool kit. But with lean, we see time and time again that the organizations that stay on the path are able to demonstrate that their gains grow as their human development progresses with more and more experience with lean tools, practices, principles, and leadership behaviors.

So, there are two lessons in the FNOK example: (1) the impact of $n/10$ kaizen event pace, and (2) the fact that you begin to get really good at this stuff only in the fifth or sixth year of a lean initiative; the gains will then accelerate through the tenth year or so.

DESIGNING IMPROVEMENT TEAMS

Over the years, the organizations in which I worked tried a wide variety of theories about who should be on a weeklong improvement team. The best practice turned out to be a team of six to nine people that included as required members:

- A supervisor from the area being studied: He or she will provide detailed knowledge of the current process, and will then own the new process after the event week.
- Two to three members from the area: They know the way the work is done today, they will be helping the rest of their team buy into the new methods after the event, and their personal kaizen event experience is also part of the long-term cultural change process. These first-level members will not only gain new problem-solving skills but also come to appreciate and support improvement in their work areas. It turns out that the most motivating way in which people can be involved with their workplace is the improvement of their own work processes. In fact, the lack of improvement to work areas and processes is usually a very large source of personal frustration every day at work.
- One or two team members who have significant prior kaizen team experience: They add efficiency to the team, both in terms of knowledge and also in terms of already believing that this lean stuff will

work. These are also the folks who will be getting a lot of event experience and who will become your own future sensei as they get their 60 to 100 event experiences over the years.

- One or two optional team members: They may not add much value to the event itself, but they will be there for their personal learning. Keep in mind, however, that too many optional team members can be distracting, due to their inexperience, so you want to limit their numbers on each team. There should be no more optional members than there are experienced lean team members.

A typical event team has a team leader and an assistant team leader. The best practice in this area is for the team leader to be a budding sensei—someone with significant lean experience in your firm—and for the assistant team leader to be the supervisor of the area. If the area supervisor becomes the team leader, he or she will tend to try to minimize the change, rather than maximize the improvement. Still, the supervisor should be close to the action during the event week, so serving as the assistant team leader works well.

In the optional team member category, consider including management and other executive staff, who can use this event to get personal experience learning to see waste and remove waste. The most successful lean organizations require all executive staff members to get a minimum number of event experiences in their first year in the firm. Part of your overall transformation plan of care (covered in Chapter 6) should be a detailed plan of how you will use each kaizen event to enable another senior executive to learn through a basic kaizen event.

Senior executives should be team members—not team leaders—when they are on a team. Senior leaders usually don't have strong enough lean skills, they usually don't know the work area very well, and the best learning experience for them is to be participating, full-time team members. The more senior the executive, the more he or she will feel it is okay to be on the team only part time. It turns out that this destroys the executive's personal learning experience, and it is also disrespectful of the rest of the team. The best practice for executives who are scheduled on a team is for them to be treated as if they are on vacation. Senior executives somehow manage to get in a few vacation weeks every year, and the organization runs just fine anyway. The event week participation needs to be treated the same way.

One other optional team member you may want to place on a team is a vendor, especially if the vendor's firm supplies material or services to the value stream you're studying. Likewise, from the other end of the value chain, you may want to ask a customer to serve on your team. Occasionally, firms will also allow individuals from other organizations interested in lean to get kaizen event experience as team members. This is not essential to your success, but it is a good way to share your learning.

KEY EVENT FAILURE MODE

Some companies hold a weeklong kaizen event, make process changes, and then do not expect to follow up in the weeks after the event, so all the required improvements do not get made. This is the most common event failure mode, at least until companies get tired of the waste inherent in the practice.

Typically, team members produce a *kaizen newspaper,* which is a list of items remaining to be completed at the end of the event week. Ninety-five percent of the changes will already have been made, but another 5 percent call for some purchased material, a bit more tool room time, and so on. It is not unusual for these items to be neglected, which is why they need to be highlighted. Although these items may seem to management like a small list of relatively unimportant items, to the people in the work area they are critical to success. They are also indicative of management's true support for the change—or lack thereof. And for those who really do not want to make any changes, this nagging list of items left undone is sufficient reason for them *not* to stick to the new improved method.

But there is also a more basic lean concept at work in the immediate time after a formal improvement event. Ohno talked about how removing a layer of waste makes the next layer more visible. Much of the system design of the lean approach is aimed at this goal; in fact, in the typical system design, the waste becomes visible by bringing the work to a stop if there was an unresolved problem. What you do during an event removes waste (things like excess inventory, excess people, and so on). After an event, in which you have made a significant improvement and moved the system much closer to true one-piece flow, you will find that the system is designed so that smaller problems that used to be hidden under excess people and inventory will now come to the surface, typically by stopping the line or the flow of value creation. In fact, the process comes to a halt for successively smaller and smaller problems. Lean is about root-cause problem solving, and the system is trying to show you the next layer of previously unidentified problems, so that you can go solve them at a root-cause level and create the next level of improvement.

Of course, when you are a normal firefighting organization, each time the system comes to a halt, it appears as though the new system does not work, but it is working to expose additional waste. This means that, for several weeks after an event, you need to keep a significant portion of your dedicated kaizen resource in the work area solving all the small problems that the system is pushing to the surface as it makes the next layer of waste visible. The good news is that this will also provide the next level of improvement. The bad news is that if you do not solve these new problems, the system will tend to come to a stop, and you will most likely go backward.

THE 3 PERCENT GUIDELINE

Another rule of thumb that results from experimenting with various levels of lean support is the *3 percent guideline*. In order to prepare for an $n/10$ pace of events, conduct the events, and then do quality follow-up and problem solving after the events, you need some dedicated resources to support the lean journey.

Personal experience has shown me that firefighting organizations are incapable of having people work part time on improvement. At various times, I have hired new members who are meant to be dedicated to improvement projects, but I found that they inevitably got sucked into the firefighting, and my carefully created improvement resource disappeared. So I learned that if I wanted to assure that some of my total organizational resource was truly dedicated to fundamental improvement, I had to have full-time folks who were not allowed to firefight. Instead, their mission was making sure that our work practices and processes were better tomorrow than they are today.

Full-time lean resources are critical when taking an organization to the next level of performance. To work on an event pace that follows the $n/10$

rule, focus on events that produce significant True North metric results. To make sure the company did not slide back to the old practices after each improvement event, I have found that the appropriate support organization is about 3 percent of the value stream, worksite, or business unit total employment. These 3 percent individuals do much of the preparation work before events, are usually team members during events (and because they will get the most event experience, they are your only real source of future sensei), and support the area supervisor for follow-up/problem solving after an event.

In fact, about half of the work of the 3 percent full-time lean time is event follow-up. After an event, the system will be pushing long-hidden problems to the surface. The area supervisor may have limited lean experience and limited problem-solving experience, and probably has a firefighting mentality. To balance this, the 3 percent provides a surge of lean problem-solving resources to respond to these hidden problems that are coming to the surface. If these skilled problem-solving resources are not in the work area in the weeks immediately after an event, the team in the area will be overwhelmed and will see the whole effort as unsuccessful. (Trust me, this no-follow-up approach is almost a 100 percent failure mode in the first couple years of most organizations' lean efforts.)

Many executives look on building up this 3 percent group as a resource drain. My view was always the opposite, because I wanted to build up a resource that I knew was going to make us better every day. Throughout my career, I found that these dedicated improvement resources were the prime source of financial improvement and, thus, were deemed to be one of our most important assets. Even executives who agree, however, have trouble figuring out how to build up this kind of resource, given day-to-day budget constraints. The answer turns out to be straightforward, albeit demanding. You use the resources you gain through productivity improvements to flesh out your dedicated lean team.

Typically, an event week might have four kaizen event teams focused on four of the key issues identified in the value stream analysis. One or two of those teams will likely focus on improving productivity in some area of the value stream. For example, at HON, in a two-year period, 49 percent of our teams (491 kaizen event teams in total) had a primary focus on the use of the standard work tool. And of the 491 total improvement teams, the average productivity gain was 45 percent. Given this, we could pretty well establish the number of people we could free up before the event even took place. Knowing that we would free up people resources with each of these kaizen events, we set a standard that for every five people we freed up through the lean effort, we would add one full-time person to the dedicated improvement team.

This basically said two things: (1) we are going to fund our improvement resource through our improvement efforts, and (2) we are going to reinvest 20 percent of our productivity savings into resources that accelerate our pace of improvement. We were able to fully fund our 3 percent dedicated team by the end of the first year of lean—without hiring anyone and without shortchanging the resources from an existing work area.

For those individuals selected to join the full-time improvement team, we selected the best person in the organization, not the actual person we had freed up that week. Instead, we used the freed-up human resource, through our redeployment process, to "pay" for dedicating the resource that we needed. You will be investing a huge amount of time and effort in each dedicated team member's personal learning, so you want to make sure each is your best and brightest. In the lean world, the definition of best and brightest is somewhat different from everyday practice. Basically, the selection criteria parallel those that Toyota uses for hiring. You want to select people who:

- Can learn new things
- Can identify and solve problems
- Work well in teams
- Can communicate well

Like many things at Toyota, this list may look simple, but it is the result of incredible careful thought and trial. For example, take the selection of people who can identify and solve problems. Toyota's experience is that those are two separate skills. In its selection process, Toyota uses simulation and other methods to find folks who can identify problems; it turns out many people do not seem to be aware of problems even when they are all around. Obviously, solving problems would be of no value if you cannot identify that there are problems to solve.

In addition, in a manufacturing organization, you may find it useful to look for associates who are tech heavy; it really helps to have a few toolmakers, a couple maintenance folks, and a few manufacturing or industrial engineers on the full-time lean team. In fact, you want about three-quarters of your typical team to be techy in this sense, because many of the problems that they must solve will involve process knowledge, tool design, and so on.

Another key question on the 3 percent guideline is who should lead this dedicated team. The answer will probably surprise you. It should be the heir apparent for the site or business unit. A fairly common failure in lean is when a general manager "gets it" and starts to build a lean learning organization. Then, five years later, this person gets promoted, and the heir apparent takes over—except that he or she has been doing another key job in the business and has not been directly involved in the lean transformation. The heir apparent will talk the talk but is not really committed to the lean transformation. The solution to this is that you take that heir apparent and make him or her the leader of the dedicated lean team, where the person will become deeply knowledgeable about the lean transformation. Taking this approach also has a great communication value at the start of your journey. Everyone usually knows who is the heir apparent anyway (or, at least, they know the couple of folks in the running for this role), and if this person is put in charge of the full-time transformation effort, you've sent a clear message that the lean transformation is very important—and we all had better pay attention.

Most organizations do the opposite and look around for someone who is simply available to put in charge of the lean effort. Well, the reality is if someone is available, there is usually a good reason for his or her being "available" and everyone in the organization is also aware of that. If you want to kill your effort before you get going, go find an "available person" to lead your dedicated team! If you want to succeed, on the other hand, commit your strongest manager to your full-time lean efforts.

Keep in mind that when you are starting the journey, you don't have the experience to deeply believe in its success, so to decide to commit your strongest managers to lead this effort full-time will be a leap of faith. But it is a very necessary one. Even if it doesn't feel "right" to put such a person in charge, it will be a decision that will pay off for years to come.

Also remember that the dedicated lean team you build will be the only people to get significant kaizen event experience, which means they will become your own internal sensei. These are people with enough lean experience to assure continuity of your improvement effort—forever.

ADMINISTRATIVE TEAMS

Teams focused on improving administrative processes are much like any other improvement team—and also different. They are similar in that they use the same tools and principles that are used to drive lean improvement in other areas. But they are different because the people doing the work think about their jobs differently.

The first thing to give some thought to is how we have organized administrative work everywhere. In manufacturing, we used to decry batch manufacturing, where we built process villages by combining all the similar machine types in separate departments, which required us to move parts between those departments to complete the assembly. In some cases, a warehouse operation had to be added between each value-adding process step. Most of the world knows this is a poor way to organize work and that it creates great waste. Generally if you move a batch operation to a Toyota flow-style operation (with five passes through each value stream to get deep lean improvement), you will get astonishing results: 90 percent less flow time and inventory, 90 percent fewer defects, 90 percent lower accident rates, and 80 percent less work.

In the same way, most companies have organized administrative work in batch style. Functional departments are akin to process villages, where the work of that functional specialty is done. But when you actually want to complete a process—to get an administrative value stream to flow—you find that you have to confront your process villages and the fact that the data you are trying to turn into information travels in boxes of data from department to department. Think, for example, about the flow of data you use to pay a vendor. It starts with a purchase order, then you get a purchase receipt at your dock, then you get a trip to the inspection function to approve the receipt, then you travel to accounting to tie all the pieces of paper together, then you usually do a rework step or two, then eventually get approval to pay (often from another department), and then you pay the bill. And almost all of these work steps go through the mail system, adding more non-value-added work. Lean folks have kaizened processes such as this, and one of the more thorough approaches has been to have a robust supply chain, where you can pay the vendor automatically upon ordering because you know all the other required actions will happen. In any case, the end result is that every administrative process is organized on batch concepts and has batch levels of *muda* (waste), meaning there is great opportunity.

In spite of all this opportunity, however, you almost never find True North metrics in administrative areas—in fact, you almost never find *any* performance metrics at all in administrative areas. What you find instead is great resistance to the idea of being measured. In operations, folks are used to the idea of their work being measured in some fashion, but as you run lean events in administrative areas, you will find that you often have trouble getting the team members to admit to their gains. They will usually be okay telling you about their quality gains, or even their throughput gains, but they almost never volunteer that they have made a productivity gain. In other words, if you drop half the steps in a process, which then leads to a halving of lead time and a halving of errors, it probably stands to reason that you will also halve the work content. But the gains tend to be hidden by the admin folks themselves. These productivity gains are there (and may even be easier to put into place than in a production area), but the concept of incorporating productivity gains into an admin area is foreign, so you have to manage the improvement process more closely than in other areas.

One idea I put into place in my companies is to have the administrative lean teams report to the controller's office. Controllers know they are not responsible for generating an outcome, but they are responsible for describing it accurately in numbers. This characteristic makes it hard for them to have teams report to them with inconsistent or incomplete results. For this reason, having the admin team report to the financial or accounting area is likely to get real measurements in place and real results achieved.

One other suggestion is to set up dedicated administrative lean teams, instead of mixing lean teams in admin and operations. In my experience, whenever I found a good team leader from operations who knew how to apply the lean tools and asked him or her to lead an admin team, they were always successful. The problem is these folks do not like working in admin areas where folks are not used to measuring their own performance, so they would keep drifting back to operations. Instead, I started setting up dedicated admin lean teams that did nothing but lean events in administrative areas. These poor folks could not run away from admin! And they got better and better at it. Another benefit of lean teams that worked only on admin areas is that the mix of skills on admin teams needed to be different from production. Where the tech skills for production involved tool making and similar skills, the tech skills that were helpful on admin teams involved folks with real knowledge of the IT system, how to change software, how the financial system really worked, and so on. They were still tech oriented, but it was "office tech."

In most manufacturing firms, at least half of the members are not in production—and usually are paid more than production workers—so you normally find that two-thirds of your employment cost and potential for productivity gains lies in the administrative processes. The net result: You cannot become a lean enterprise without getting deep into administrative lean work—period!

When we checked the results of our administrative teams at HON/HNI, we found that they averaged a 33 percent reduction in cycle time for the process/value stream, a 46 percent reduction in the number of steps, and an 85 percent increase in productivity. Powerful stuff!

REDEPLOYMENT

Redeployment is an interesting lean practice area. Typical of many Toyota-like things, the right approach is just the opposite of what you might normally do. Think about how companies usually handle redeployment of personnel. Let's say you have just bought a new IT system or a new super-wonderful machine, and now you can run the area with one less person. How do we select the person to redeploy? Most managers have been taught to optimize that team and that means that if you can now run the team with one less person, you would naturally select the worst performer and move him or her out of the area. (In fact, some managers go so far as to give a great review to a poor performer, hoping that some other area will hire that person away.)

Even though team members knew this person was the low performer on their team, they still had worked together for a number of years (perhaps even met some of their family) and don't want to see them "get hurt." Likewise, the low performer has an equally traumatic experience; this person knows he or she was the low performer on the team and is afraid of getting fired. So morale suffers, everywhere.

The Toyota practice is simple. Instead of moving out the low performer, you move out your best performer. Toyota's logic goes something like this: We have kaizened the work process in the area, allowing us to free up a member for redeployment. In doing this, we have solved some quality problems, made the work more repeatable, and made it easier to do. So we do not really need the same level of skills that we needed before the improvement. So let's take the best member of the team and redeploy him or her. This person is likely to see a move to a new area as an interesting, perhaps challenging, change. And everyone knows management is not going to be firing the best person on the team, so morale holds up well. And, of course, all the other areas of the company are happy to accept this new person onto their team, so this person is easy to redeploy. If you don't have a current job opening today, this person will make a valuable contribution as a temporary member of the full-time kaizen team. When a job opens up that fits, the employee will have increased lean skills and become even more excited about being part of your organization's team. Although this seems sensible, keep in mind that this is exactly the opposite of the standard practice that all of your people have been trained in. So, as my Japanese sensei said to me, "Easy to say ... hard to do!"

OTHER LEAN TRAINING

You have seen the primacy of the *jishukin* or event format as a method of achieving results (see Chapter 4), developing lean learning, and building a stronger culture. There is, however, a role for a limited amount of the traditional types of training for lean. There are really three principal target groups:

- **All employees:** This group should get an introduction to lean principles and concepts. This may be as little as one day's worth of training, perhaps spread over several weeks/months. This may be classroom-style training (taught by members of the dedicated lean team), or it may be simulation exercises (there are a number of good ones, which help in teaching the basic idea of flow versus batch), or you might do learning maps. At HON/HNI, we designed (with the help of Root Learning Inc.) learning maps to cover the basic principles of lean, basic financial literacy, and so on. A *learning map* is a custom-designed game board that turns the learning experience into a game. The topic of the learning map can be a variety of things. At

HON/HNI, we developed learning maps that taught basic principles of lean, basic financial literacy, and industry dynamics to support the need for change.

- **The dedicated lean team:** This group needs an introduction to its new role and what work it will be doing. This training often comes from an outside sensei group that might be teaching your organization the new lean knowledge.
- **Senior leadership:** This group should get a deeper understanding of lean. There are a number of approaches. One that has worked involves book reviews of key lean books, where a chapter is reviewed and discussed at each monthly or weekly executive team meeting. Another is conducting lean leadership workshops with outside sensei. But just keep in mind that the greatest deep learning will come from personal experience on an event team—that is, learning to see waste and remove it.

SUMMARY

Experience has shown that if you want to sustain significant improvement gains over the long term, you will need to do the following:

- Establish a regular pace of process improvement activity at a level that seems high to the folks who are not yet part of an improvement culture.
- Build a dedicated support group of your best folks, who will help sustain this high level of improvement activity and also be your future sensei.
- Be thoughtful about the makeup of each improvement team and its goals.
- Give special focus as to how you organize your administrative lean efforts.
- Develop a robust redeployment process that provides the human resource to support your lean efforts and the productivity gains to improve business results.

6

Strategic Organizational Practices

Governance is *the* key issue with lean. Although individual lean concepts and tools are easy to understand, to be truly successful in the application of these concepts and tools, the majority of the organization must change the way it looks at work. And this is hard to do, because we have spent our careers building an image of how work should be organized and done. This fundamental change in the way you see work—and how you think it should be organized—is the most basic change needed to be successful at lean. And so far, the vast majority of the organizations that start on the lean transformation journey are not successful at making this transition.

UNDERSTANDING GOVERNANCE

Governance is about the governors—the leaders of the organization and what they do. The track record so far shows that normal corporate governance practices are insufficient for the challenges of a lean transformation. Even Toyota, which is today managed by the fourth generation of leaders who have practiced the business system they have built, does not provide a particularly helpful benchmark. Toyota represents the end state that you can aspire to, but simply mimicking what it does today will not get your organization moving in the direction of successful transformation. The current generation of Toyota leadership is long removed from the change-management practices needed to start a successful transformation. Toyota is doing an amazing job of sustaining its culture, but the company cannot show many recent examples of outside firms that it has been able to get on a similar path to building a sustainable lean learning culture.

If you look outside Toyota for models of successful transformation—organizations whose financial metrics have demonstrated that their lean practices generate additional customer value on a continuing basis—the list gets pretty small. Many organizations have made incremental gains, but few have shown that they can get continuous gains, and fewer still have demonstrated that they can do this on a regular basis with new companies they acquire or create. In this regard, Danaher is perhaps the closest to the mark. Danaher has had compounded increases in earnings in the mid-20 percent range since starting its lean efforts in 1987. And every year, the company acquires new, non-lean organizations that it gets onto this path. Danaher is still learning and building its culture, but some of its practices are worth thinking about.

IMMERSION

Lean learning is hands-on learning that comes from the personal struggle of applying new concepts and tools to your own workplace, and then learning from this struggle. Successful organizations have developed an approach to get their leaders new knowledge that changes the way they view work. For senior leaders, it is not necessary for them to get to the point where they are experts at the application of a certain lean tool or deeply knowledgeable in the full range of lean tools. The real key for senior leaders is to get just enough personal experience to allow them to begin to see waste in the work that surrounds them every day. Once they begin to see the seven wastes in the daily work that is all around them, they have the incentive and motivation to attack this waste and reduce it. For leaders, learning to see waste is the key.

At HON/HNI, new managers, whether internal promotions or external hires, get four weeklong kaizen event experiences in their first year on the job. Leaders first participate in a standard-work event in a production area, because it is typically easier to see waste in a production process than in other processes. This first up-close experience with waste will often be an eye-opener in terms of being shocked at how much waste is in the area studied and also that half of that waste can be removed within the same week.

In the second weeklong event, leaders participate in a value-stream-analysis event, in which they begin to see waste in terms of quality, time consumption, and productivity at a high level—sort of a 20,000-foot view of waste. This is then followed by a weeklong administrative standard-work event, which will open their eyes to what waste looks like in purely administrative processes. A fourth weeklong event is required with the 3P tool (see the Foundations section to this book), which is used to invent new product and process designs, and also to align process and product development with lean practices. So HON/HNI requires four weeks of kaizen-event-based immersion as the starting point.

With this as the foundation, HON/HNI requires every manager to get an additional two full weeks of event experiences every year thereafter. It "encourages" this by making achievement of two additional weeks of event experience a condition for eligibility in that year's bonus program.

At Danaher, the immersion process for new leaders is a formal thirteen-week process. In the process, about two-thirds of the time is spent on kaizen event teams operating in a variety of different Danaher businesses. About one-third of the time is spent on lean governance, benchmarking good lean operations and management practice at various locations, joining strategy deployment sessions, and going to a week of formal Danaher Business System (DBS) Leadership Training. The immersion is conducted under the guidance of a personal mentor (a senior Danaher manager who is deeply knowledgeable and committed to DBS) who constructs the specific plan for the new manager and coaches him or her through the thirteen weeks of immersion.

The point is that it will not be sufficient to think you can transform leaders with a single-week's time commitment or only in classrooms. Instead, the first critical step in governance is to develop a plan for how you will immerse senior leaders in a lean approach to organizing your work. This is the key to success, and you will need to put more effort into it than you think.

GUIDING COALITION

John Kotter, who writes about change management, talks about establishing a guiding coalition to help a CEO guide the lean change. A *guiding coalition* is the senior management group that will guide the transformation process for the whole enterprise. The thought here is around several key issues:

- A change in culture will need more than one senior person who is working to imbed the new culture into the organization.
- The lean path is not perfectly clear, so the input of multiple senior leaders will help with midcourse corrections.
- Any key player who is on the outside looking in will tend to fight the process.

Thus, a good initial task for the guiding coalition is to develop the immersion experience that will be used for their own education, as well as for other leaders, as the lean process expands.

This is the point at which organizations often implement their transformation value stream analysis (TVSA; see the Introduction to this book). The goal of TVSA is to take a look at the basic business strategy of the organization, look at how the organization's key value streams (at the highest level) fulfill key stakeholder needs and enable the strategy, assess lean potential to accelerate and deepen the strategic impact, and then begin to build the transformation plan. Part of a TVSA is also to determine how to track and measure the True North metrics and how these metrics will tie to financial performance.

After that, the initial improvement focus needs to be selected. This should be an area (a value stream) that is significant to the company, ideally one that has potential to grow with improved lead times, quality, and so on. But most important is that it is an area where the local leaders really are leaders—individuals who will commit the extra personal effort needed to experiment with new lean ways and bring their team along on the often-confusing and difficult lean journey. I suggest that the most important criteria for the first targeted value stream focus area is the quality of leadership in that value stream. A good leader can make even a poor plan succeed, and a poor leader can kill the best of plans.

There are a few things to keep in mind as you start. You select a key value stream based on the quality of its leadership and its importance or impact. Then you need to assure basic improvement resources. Three key steps should be taken:

- You need a sensei to teach your organization lean tools/concepts and to coach your team on the leadership issues.

- In the value stream you select, you need to dedicate 3 percent of the total headcount to ongoing support for improvement of this value stream (see Chapter 5). By initiating the 3 percent rule only for a single value stream, the number of people dedicated to improvement starts low and grows as each new value stream starts up. But after the first value stream is operating, it will be generating a flow of improvement results that will cover the cost of starting up of the next value stream, so you really only invest in folks to start the initial value stream—that is, future resources are paid for by productivity gains and redeployment from initial value streams.
- You start improvement events at a pace that will build sufficient gains to have impact, will build experience (lean learning) fast enough to grow your own future sensei, and will show the long-term potential to build a new culture as all members get personal experience with learning to see and remove waste.

Experience has shown that this pace is related to population, which makes the $n/10$ rule (see Chapter 5) about right. Typically, it is important to have a regular rhythm of at least one event-week per month. A less frequent event pace will lead to too much lost momentum between events and insufficient impact on results in performance, learning, and culture building.

Also keep in mind the rule of 5X (see Chapter 4). Once you get through the first pass of improvement in the initial value stream, keep your 3 percent dedicated resources there and start the next pass of improvement, at the same time using some of the savings/freed up resources to fund the establishment of an improvement organization for another value stream. You will, of course, need to prove to yourself and your company that the five passes of improvement are not only real, but also that the results are often greatest in the fourth or fifth passes. These types of results are just too far away from everyday experience to believe it until you prove it to your own organization with your own work. But this focus on multiple passes of lean improvement will build this value stream into the *model value stream*—the area where the results are compelling to all who see them and where the culture becomes so established that it will sustain the improvement through generations.

Too many firms set up dedicated full-time lean staff to support their lean transformations, but then allow these folks to just get wrapped up in administration and never get any real learning from personal event experience. This approach never works. The full-time resources for improvement must be required to get monthly event experience so they grow their own learning of what waste is and how to remove it. The vast majority of the dedicated lean resources should be at the level of the individual value streams, focused on continually hitting True North improvement metrics for their value stream.

You may want to establish a transformation mission control room, where the guiding coalition will normally meet. The room should also feature a hard copy of the TVSA, the Total Plan of Care (an outline of key steps in the transformation journey), the personal immersion/development plans for key leaders, the strategy deployment plan, the initial value stream analysis and plan, charts of True North Metric performance, and so on. And all this material should be visually displayed on the walls of the mission control room.

COMMUNICATION

You really cannot overcommunicate when undertaking any large change in your organization. One way to think about communication is to review some of the data from a study of sales presentations, which noted that three days after a presentation, you can recall only about 11 percent of the information presented. So if you think your message is important, think about repeating it about ten times. We tend to think, "I told them that already!" when we probably should be thinking, "They remembered only 11 percent of what I told them, so how will I get the other 89 percent across?"

It is good to repackage the message several times and use different mediums. Make full use of company newsletters, company video messages, and every other possible avenue of communicating the basics. And the basics are:

- Why do we need to change (what are the key competitive or customer drivers)?
- Why have we chosen this path?
- How will this path work?
- What will each person's role be in this transformation?

You may also want to try some new forms of communication, as discussed in the two following sections.

Lean Simulation

About 99 percent of lean education will come from hands-on experience (see Figure 6.1). However, the 1 percent that comes from traditional educational approaches is still important. The whole organization needs to get some basic idea of what lean is all about. A basic introduction to lean is a solid step. Another good step is to take groups of members through a *lean simulation*, which is a mock-up of a work area that demonstrates basic batch practices, and then shows the evolution to flow.

A lean simulation usually takes about four hours to conduct. When done well, it introduces the key principles of lean—flow, pull, value streams, and so on—and it usually does so in a way that words cannot do. Well-done simulations give participants a mental picture of the waste in your current batch approach and show the potential for improvement in quality, lead time, and productivity. It is really great to see someone "get it" after participating in a simulation.

Strategy Deployment

One lean strategic organizational process is *hoshin kanri,* which is also called *hoshin* planning, management by policy, and policy deployment.

FIGURE 6.1
Team doing a lean simulation.

(Simpler Consulting uses the term *strategy deployment,* as discussed in the Introduction to this book.) The basic idea of strategy deployment is to review key strategic efforts for the next year, identify how lean improvement can accelerate and enable these efforts, set True North goals to support the strategic direction, establish the pace and pattern of improvement effort for the year to achieve these goals, and then establish a monthly review process.

Most monthly review meetings or monthly operations meetings are focused on financial metrics and have a budgetary outlook. Strategy deployment will do a similar thing but with a focus on improvement—the process to assure that our performance tomorrow is better than our performance today, forever.

With strategy deployment, an annual effort is undertaken to set improvement goals for the organization that will enable the chosen strategic initiatives, and then break these improvement goals down to each lower level of the organization, and, at the value-adding level, develop the improvement work plan to meet these goals. Typical questions include:

- What value streams will we have to improve to meet this year's goals?
- How many improvement events will likely be needed to achieve this?
- What will the focus of those events be?
- Who will support those events?

This annual planning effort will not detail exactly what improvement work you will be doing six months from now, but it will give the folks who need to drive the value stream improvement efforts a good idea of the pace of improvement work they will need to sustain to hit the overall goals.

After the annual improvement plan is set, monthly follow-up meetings are used to assess progress and share learning. Typically, each value stream team reviews the results of the prior month, taking a fast look at the *rate* of improvement—in other words, did the team hit the improvement for human development, quality, lead time, and productivity? Reviewing this information takes up about 10 percent of the meeting time. Instead of spending time talking about the result numbers, this meeting spends time talking about what *drives* the numbers.

So after the short review of "did we hit our improvement targets this past month," the value stream team reviewed the key improvement events implemented in the past month and the key lessons learned from these. If a goal wasn't met, the value stream team would identify additional lean-event efforts to catch up to that goal. Next, the value stream team would review the key events planned for the upcoming month and estimate whether this will be sufficient to meet the month's improvement goals.

This dialogue provides great learning for the whole organization. The lessons learned can be shared from one team to another, and management can help identify possible corrective action steps to get back on track when an improvement target has been missed. The purpose of the meeting is to spend the time learning about what is working and talking about corrective action, as opposed to spending time reviewing the numbers. And keep focused on the here and now: Did we make it last month? If not, what are we doing about it? What have we learned? Will we make it this month? If so, how? If not, do other folks on the team have ideas on how to accelerate the improvement pace?

At some of the initial meetings, you may need to use a timer, allowing a set time for each value stream review: world class is five minutes per review, but my best was about fifteen minutes per review. People have a huge tendency to ramble and not focus on key issues, so a timer, combined with the knowledge that there is a very strict time limit and that certain topics must be covered in that time limit, can change this rambling to a tight focus. You will also find that the meetings become more efficient each year, such that you will have a much better process after three or four years.

When you first start strategy deployment, it can seem kind of clunky. But one of the first things you see is that in the week before the monthly meeting, there is a huge flurry of improvement work going on, which means that even if you're still in a firefighting culture, at least the team is focused on improvement for some of their time. This flurry of improvement focus is worth the effort of the strategy deployment process, in and of itself.

ANTIBODIES

Taiichi Ohno, the lean guru at Toyota, used to note that every organization had inside of it antibodies, just as the human body does. When a change or infection tries to enter the body, the *antibodies* do two things: they get really active fighting off this new thing and they also multiply. They add converts to their effort. This is normal. In fact, the stronger the corporate culture, the stronger the antibodies; the antibodies are there to protect the existing corporate culture.

You have undoubtedly noticed that there is often not a clear description of the corporate culture when you first join an organization, but that, over time, you learn the "rules." Well, the folks that teach the corporate culture are the antibodies. They are usually respected and long-term members of the organization.

The problem, of course, comes about when the organization needs to change. During times of significant change, the antibodies—who, again, tend to be some of your most respected and experienced members— become the folks who try to prevent improvement and change. When these antibodies emerge, leadership needs to address them.

Antibodies exist in every organization and will automatically resist anything as radical as a lean transformation. And they will do so with the best of intentions. From their perspective, the historic success of the organization was based on doing things a certain way, so changing how things are done risks everything. And the more successful the organization, the stronger the antibodies and the harder the task to get any new direction moving.

Toyota has occasionally depicted the presence of antibodies as a normal distribution curve (see Figure 6.2), with the tails on each side representing either the antibodies (poor zone) or the *change agents* (excellent zone), who are those key few leaders who are attempting to move the organization in the new direction. You absolutely need to support the change agents, but this is only half the answer. If you support the change agents and start moving in new directions, a few interesting phenomena will happen.

First, the antibodies will get more active (informally at coffee breaks, for example) in resisting the new direction. They will also talk more members, those who are close to their views, into becoming new antibodies. The end result is that if you only support the change agents, you end up with turmoil as the mass of members in the middle hears two opposite messages about where the organization should be going—both messages coming from respected members of the organization. This is where leaders have to lead. The best thing to do is to make it clear that (1) the organization is going to go on this journey, (2) the role of every member is to work to support this change, and (3) those who will not or cannot change need to think about finding another organization where they would be more comfortable.

The faster you identify each true antibody and address him or her (see Figure 6.3), the fewer antibodies you will have to address in the end. Over

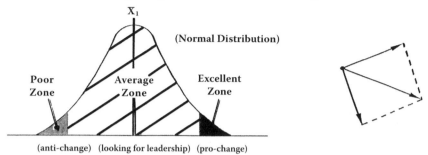

FIGURE 6.2
Toyota change model 1.

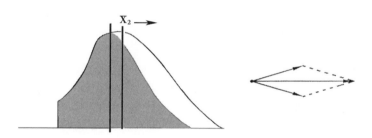

FIGURE 6.3
Toyota change model 2.

time, as folks gain personal experience with the process, most of the significant antibodies will most likely buy-in, but you must address the first few early so they don't multiply. If they do multiply, you will never be able to stay on track long enough to convert them, so early action is key.

One caution: When you start on this journey, it is new to everyone, which means that any thinking person will initially question the direction. This may make everyone appear to be an antibody. The difference is that real antibodies never accept the answers to any of their questions and don't want to participate in the process. It does not take long to see the true antibodies, as opposed to those who have genuine questions about the company's new direction.

LEAN YEAR BY YEAR

A well-planned and aggressively led lean transformation will follow a regular cultural transformation pace over the first four years or so.

Year One

When you start the lean journey, the idea is totally new to your whole organization, so the concepts take time to sink in. However, at the end of the first year of your lean transformation effort, you will be impressed by the improvements made in specific events and in some targeted value streams. You will see individual results that look promising, but you may not see that the enterprise financial metrics have moved as much as you had expected. Overall progress will likely be slower than you hoped for.

You will see a lot of "two steps forward, and one step back" experiences in that first year. This is a byproduct of the nature of hands-on learning, because your improvement teams are totally new to both the ideas of lean and the lean tools, so they make mistakes trying to interpret how to apply ideas like one-piece flow. In addition, the poor follow-up practices that exist in the firefighting culture at most companies keeps you from maintaining and sustaining all the improvement. The end result is that by the end of the first successful year of a lean transformation, most of your members will still be confused by the new approach or upset by the pace and magnitude of change. Unlike most corporate initiatives in which by year's end you expect to be able to declare victory, you will not see that with a lean transformation.

It is also worth noting that, by the end of the first year, less than 20 percent of your organization will have actually experienced lean work in their areas. So most of the organization will still be on the outside looking in, and this group is usually not very supportive.

Year Two

The second year is usually the year of major resistance. The antibodies that see the lean effort continue into a second year (when most programs in the past have ended) get reenergized to kill it off before it can really hurt the organization. Yet your change agents will still be inexperienced, and every time they make a mistake in trying to apply the new principles, your remaining antibodies will highlight the mistake.

By the end of the second year, you will be impacting value streams that represent 30 to 40 percent of the organization, which means the majority of your organization still will not have direct learning experience about lean. A member survey given at the end of a second year of a successful lean journey will probably say something like, "The jury is still out on this lean thing."

Year Three

The third year is a year of consolidation. Managers and full-time lean resources are gaining experience with the process. Individual events have more "two steps forward and *no* falling back" impacts. By the end of the third year, the compounding of results in quality, lead times, and productivity/cost will be large enough to demonstrate that the process is truly successful. Also by the end of the third year, your member survey might say something like, "We are making great progress—but I wonder when we will be done."

Year Four

The fourth year is characterized by "change" having gradually become the new norm. The processes of continuous improvement and continuous change are gradually becoming institutionalized by the end of the fourth year. You can feel and see tremendous positive momentum building in the organization. You may still have not touched 20 percent or so of the organization with lean efforts, but you can see that you are creating a new culture—a true learning organization that can improve forever. Your end-of-year-four member survey would change again; instead of members wondering when the process will be done, they start to hope that it can go on forever.

Most leaders think that they can get to the year-four state in one year. I have never seen anyone be able to do that, even in the best-led lean efforts. So it is good to realize that there will be tough sledding for much more than a year. If you are on track, you will be seeing results that will be positive, accumulating new skills within the organization, and building new cultural norms all along the way. But it will take about four full years for the best-led lean effort to begin to be established as the new way of doing things. After all, you can't expect to build a new culture in just a couple of years!

SUMMARY

All of this comes together as a new way of running your enterprise—in other words, you establish a new management system, like the Toyota Production System or the Danaher Business System. Although you can look at models from other companies, you have to build the system yourself. And this takes time and energy.

Most corporation leaders have been trained to manage. We were taught the virtues of delegation. We have degrees called masters of business administration, which focus on *administration*. Most of us were not taught how to lead, that is, how to take an organization in new directions. This means that our model of how to manage is not particularly useful when we actually want to successfully transform an organization. The model we need instead for this is true leadership—a willingness to demonstrate that we do not have all the answers, a willingness to go to the *gemba* (workplace) and learn how it actually works, a willingness to admit that we have to gather new knowledge and hone new skills to succeed. Most senior leaders feel that others expect them to know the answers, but with lean, the key to success is to know the questions and be willing to pursue the answers diligently.

7

Building a Lean Culture

Now for the hard part: lean culture. Over my thirty years as a student of lean transformation, my path of learning has progressed in the way that it does for most people. For years, I was focused on learning about the *tools* of lean. How do you set up reduction? How do you use standard work? How do you analyze a value stream? There was a lot to learn, and it seemed like every time I thought I had something down, I learned some new aspect of it or discovered an entirely new tool that I hadn't known existed. So I lived in the world of lean tools for a long time.

As I struggled to get results from these lean tools, I started to add knowledge and with that knowledge began to develop approaches to getting results from the tools—what you might think of as good lean *practices*. The learning of lean practices has, for me, been both haphazard and slow, mostly through trial and error, with multiple trials and many errors before I found practices that worked well and consistently.

Along with learning about lean tools and the learning or invention of lean practices, there was also a point at which I began to *believe* in the core principles of lean—flow, pull, focus on value, and so on. These concepts are all remarkably easy to talk about, but are incredibly difficult to practice. My own belief in the core principles of lean came gradually. At various times, I could look back and recognize the point at which I started to believe in any one of the core principles of lean.

It gradually dawned on me that this lean stuff was valuable only if it was a long-term organizational practice—that is, if it became the new way of running the enterprise, if it became the new company *culture*. Being an operating manager, the idea of thinking about culture did not come to me right away. But, over time, it became obvious that all the rest of my learning was *muda* (waste) if it just disappeared when the personal push or energy behind the effort went away. Eventually, the focus of my learning was to study the culture that sustains lean transformations, and this has been my focus for the past dozen years.

DEFINING CULTURE

Perhaps it is good to go over this word *culture*. An organizational culture is defined by the behaviors or habits of its leaders; in other words, the culture is formed by what these leaders *do*. "What they do" is essential to the company's success, and when you add lots of these "what they dos" together, you see the fabric of a new culture.

My learning in this area started by observing individual leadership practices that were different from typical Western practice. Originally, I did not see that these were part of some larger fabric of overall practice, which they are.

One example is selection processes. I've worked at companies where we used to joke that our "selection process" was that we held a mirror up to a person's mouth: If his or her breath fogged the mirror, we would hire them! It was meant as a joke, but like most jokes, it was based on a strong element of truth; we weren't looking for a whole lot more than a living, breathing human being.

So as part of my benchmarking, I decided to review the Toyota selection process, which includes about a dozen key steps that take a full week of time on the part of the applicant. The Toyota process includes not only the normal hiring stuff, but also groups of applicants doing simulations of problems in the workplace, doing simulations of the actual work to be done, being team interviewed and rated by a team of assessors, and so on. So the process looked pretty complex and was about 100 times as demanding as our normal practice. And what did this rigorous process select for? Just four things. The whole process worked to identify individuals who:

- Liked to learn new things
- Could identify and solve problems (recall that these are two separate skills)

- Work well in teams
- Communicate well

The contrast between the simplicity and focus of the selection goals, and the exhaustive process to assess these characteristics was surprising to me. It was a classic of many things "Toyota." It was an opposite of traditional leadership behavior, where we draw up a long list of desired traits without having any process to figure out whether we got them. Most company managers look for people who had done this kind of work before, which was the easy way to be sure they could do the work. But Toyota has a preference for people who have not had prior experience in this kind of business (because then they would not have to unlearn bad habits before they could start learning good ones). Toyota is not looking for the strongest people, the fastest people, or the smartest people but for people who can work together as a team to make improvement. I'm paraphrasing here, but I heard someone at Toyota say something like this that brings their human development system into perspective: "Most companies produce average results by hiring the smartest people, but allowing them to work with broken processes. We produce excellent results from average people who are focused on continually improving our processes." Which system do you think will win most often?

As I tried to build organizational buy-in for a new, exhaustive selection process, what seemed to help folks understand the huge time investment was to contrast it with our typical capital purchase process. In most organizations, if you make a million-dollar investment in new capital equipment, you have a study done by some technical group, then this study is reviewed by management, then the study is analyzed by financial folks, until the proposal starts to go up the approval ladder, with reviews and signatures at each management level and on to the group president or CEO level. We had hundreds of hours of evaluation for a million-dollar capital investment. Yet, when we hire someone, it is with the expectation that he or she will spend a full career with us—and we certainly will spend well over a million dollars in total compensation over the time of that one person's career—yet we typically spend almost no time working to improve the quality of this decision.

See how this way of thinking is a fundamentally different culture (Figure 7.1)?

FIGURE 7.1
Learning about leadership and culture.

THE BUILDING BLOCKS OF LEAN/TOYOTA CULTURE

I have found it hard to learn about Toyota culture. Partly, this is because I have not actually worked inside Toyota. But I have also found that the way people get introduced to the culture inside Toyota is so subtle that most people who worked at another culture before joining Toyota did not contrast the new way people interacted.

It is usually only the folks who worked in a U.S. firm, worked for Toyota for at least a decade, and then chose to leave who have come to understand the contrast between working at Toyota and working almost anywhere else. From talking with these folks and studying everything available to outsiders about Toyota behavior/culture, I have built up a list of observations. I know the list is incomplete because every once in a while I discover a new behavior/habit/leadership practice that is built into the way things are done at Toyota and *not* built into the way we usually do things. But here is the list, as of today, of lean's core values and leadership behaviors.

Serve the Customer

Most firms say they serve the customer. Most do not practice it, at least not consistently. At Toyota, this mantra is the starting point. All actions are first evaluated in terms of their impact on the customer. Of course, Toyota has profit goals, but it recognizes that the key to success is satisfied customers. The goal is to maximize customer satisfaction, while minimizing the cost or waste to satisfy those customers. Profit is what is left after serving customers in the least wasteful way. All kaizen is customer focused. Seems simple, but keeping this goal in front of everyone, every day, on every decision, is a massive task that requires enormous leadership focus and commitment.

Seek What's Right, Regardless

At Toyota, there is a premium on integrity. There is a basic understanding that if you cannot trust the information used in the organization, you cannot possibly provide the best value to the customer. And there is a premium on true courage. At HON/HNI we used to call it *active honesty*. The idea was that true integrity was not only "not lying," but it was also speaking out with the truth, even when the truth would have negative consequences. Another way to think of this is *courageous integrity*. One example of this is the Toyota practice of "bad news first," where the opportunity to improve is focused on before accolades are given.

Decide Carefully, Implement Quickly

There is an interesting contrast here. Non-lean companies are usually rushing to a solution—without spending time getting to a root cause—so the solution turns out to be a Band-Aid®, and the company faces the same issue over and over and over again.

At Toyota, there is a deep respect for understanding the problem before seeking the solution. One way of thinking about this is the practice of using the work group to address any problem in the workplace by asking why five times in a row to find the underlying cause for the problem. Solving this underlying problem will keep the surface problem from ever recurring. This is the kind of thinking that allows "average people to build great processes that achieve superior results." Another example of this decide-carefully-implement-quickly approach is the use of A3 problem solving. This is a visual approach to problem solving the typically involves using one sheet of paper that includes nine boxes or steps. Its aim is to make sure you have asked the right question to truly understand the problem, *before* you jump to implementation.

And walking through the logic of the A3—what Toyota folks call *A3 Thinking*—will build a solid solution approach that you can implement quickly and only once. This is typical Toyota style: Focus on spending a lot more time than you think you have time to spend at the front end of the process/project, and reap huge rewards by eliminating the rework that you get from trying to implement surface solutions or half-thought-through solutions.

Candidly Admit Imperfections

This one is huge. From my observation, it is, in fact, the cultural cornerstone. The basic idea is that all improvement starts with humility. Right away, this is another opposite from non-lean cultures. When you ask senior managers of non-lean businesses about the value of being humble, they really tend to think you may have lost your mind. We need to be proud! We can't be humble about who we are and what our organization does!

But how does any improvement start? It starts with recognition that something could be better. The foundation of this is the idea of humility. If you are humble about your success, you are open to seeing ways that it can be improved. The opposite of humility is arrogance, which can almost always be traced to the downfall of any organization. With a humble outlook, you are open to *hansei,* a deep reflection on both your current approach and the approach others have to a similar situation. From hansei, you move to a challenge to improve to the highest level in this area. And from the challenge comes the breakthrough level of improvement. So there is a causal link from humility to hansei to challenge to improvement. This attitude can be seen in comments from everyone at Toyota. For example, David Absher, a maintenance supervisor at TMMC (Georgetown, KY), commented, "We are nowhere near excellent, but we are on that journey." You can see the attitude of humility, the sense that there has been hansei, the view that a challenge has been set, and the assurance that the improvement process is under way. A few years ago, Fujio Cho, chairman of Toyota, was speaking at an annual meeting of the global automotive industry in Traverse City, Michigan. The CEOs of the major global automotive firms were each giving a talk, and they were saying what you would expect: They noted the progress their firm was making, how good their products were becoming, and so on. You have heard the talk a hundred times. Then Cho started to speak, his comments went something like this: "We see things differently at Toyota. The sense of crisis that we feel stems from our fear that we have not kept up." I cannot imagine a non-lean CEO making those comments, because they feel they need to be beating their chests in public, that their teams would be discouraged if we talked about shortcomings. But Cho talks to the world, and especially his own team, about the need to accelerate improvement and the concern about losing momentum while his firm's stock market capitalization is roughly equivalent to that of the whole rest of the global automotive industry combined.

Speak Honestly and with Deep Respect

One key part of lean culture is the value of speaking with integrity, even if it hurts. The deep respect part is equally important. The point is that, as a supervisor, you have to build the personal skill to be able to honestly assess strengths and weaknesses of your team members, and then, most difficult of all, review shortcomings in a way that shows deep respect for the individual and helps each accept a review of shortcomings as something positive. Sounds simple, but it's really hard.

Go See and Listen to Learn (*Genchi Gembutsu*)

Toyota has a strong bias to always go to where the work is occurring and observe what is happening there. The idea is to truly understand the problem. There is a belief at Toyota that reports and meetings that occur away from the actual site of the work being discussed will lead to incorrect assumptions and conclusions. The Japanese phrase *genchi gembutsu* means roughly "the real thing, in the real place."

There are stories of new hotshot university graduates being hired at Toyota, and then spending their first full day in "the Ohno circle." This is a chalk circle of a couple feet in diameter drawn on the workplace floor, where the newly minted graduate would spend his or her first full day—with no instructions. The new grad, however, would eventually start to observe the work that was going on around him or her and, if he or she was good, would eventually notice some aspect of the work that did not seem to make sense or did not look efficient. At the end of the day, Ohno would ask for the grad's observations and test his or her ability to observe real work, in the actual workplace, and see possibilities for improvement. This was the first step for future leaders—personally building the skill to see waste in the work that surrounds them. This was boot camp for future lean practitioners.

This attitude can be seen in how Absher describes Toyota's Georgetown, Kentucky, operation, where there are about 7,000 total members. "It is like we have 7,000 industrial engineers working here. They see waste, and they know how to remove it." That is the culture you want to build—where your human resource really is your resource.

Another example of understanding the real workplace can be seen in product development practices. As Yugi Yokaya, chief engineer for the Sienna minivan noted, "I must drive through all fifty states, all Canadian provinces, and Mexico, seeing firsthand how people use minivans." The real thing, in the real place.

Deliver on Meaningful Challenges

There is a strong fundamental belief at Toyota that people are at their highest state and create their best results when they are responding to a significant challenge. You will find this reference to "challenge" through-out Toyota's management practice. The idea is that a significant challenge will energize a team and will be the source of motivation to achieve a breakthrough result. It has to be a goal that can be achievable, but also one that will not be easily achievable. As Teriyuki Minoura, president of TMMNA (Toyota Motor Manufacturing North America), noted, "It is a basic characteristic of human beings that they develop wisdom from being put under pressure." Or as Absher describes it, "We set really high targets, and then try like crazy to get there. If we don't reach a target, we try to figure out why we fell short. Is there anything we can do to take another step?"

Does your maintenance supervisor think like this? Does *everyone* in your organization think like this? Keep in mind that you create diamonds (in this case, great leaders) from coal (average material) by thoughtfully putting it under great heat and pressure.

Another example comes from a challenge that current CEO Katsuaki Watanabe has given to the whole of Toyota (which I've paraphrased): "We must design a car that can cross the whole world with a single tank of gas, that will clean the air as it operates, and that will never harm either a passenger or a pedestrian." This is a challenge that will stretch the creativity of the whole of the global Toyota organization. By stretching their creativity, Toyota expects to achieve a breakthrough in automotive design. They probably will not meet this exact goal, but the challenge of working at it will create solutions that no one can envision today—Toyota has set True North for car design—and will work diligently to close the gap every year. Senior business leaders often shy away from setting this kind of challenge, but thoughtful challenges provide the most inspiring work for human beings.

Be a Mentor and a Role Model

The following Toyota expression is perhaps the most fundamental expression of its culture: "We build people before we build cars." Toyota takes this seriously. The first role of anyone in any level of supervision is to "build people." And the key to building people is careful mentoring. Because the building of people is job one at Toyota, the skill of mentoring is taken very seriously. One interesting aspect is the way mentoring is assessed. Non-lean managers usually spend a lot of time trying to impress their bosses—carefully preparing presentations to demonstrate how smart they are and how they did a really great job. Of course, this is all *muda* (waste)! A basic approach at Toyota is that mentoring is a given; in fact, you cannot be promoted until you have demonstrated that you are a solid mentor. And the *only* way you can demonstrate this skill is with a result—that is, the personal growth of the people on your team, those you have mentored. You do not demonstrate this by *talking* about how good you are at mentoring. In fact you have to be silent and let your students speak for you, by demonstrating how much they have learned, by showing the challenges they have met, and presenting the improvements they have made.

To get consideration for promotion, you have to have the people on your team demonstrate how they have grown. Think about this for a minute. Just how powerful and transformational would it be to have a culture where the only way you could look good was through the success of those you mentored? It is hard to imagine the cultural impact of this one leadership behavior alone.

THE ACTION PLAN

One of the complications for non-Toyota companies trying to institute a lean vision is that we have to start where we are, with the cultures that we have. And it turns out that some of the behaviors that are part of the where-we-are may make it difficult to actually get there.

When you go back in history you find that in the early days of building a lean culture and lean business system, it was generally not possible to just talk folks into doing it—they had to be "strongly encouraged" to start the journey. Ohno noted at one point that only strong management leadership will get the organization on the new path when he said, "I utilized my authority to the fullest extent."[1] From hearing various stories about Ohno, you begin to realize that if he said he used his authority to "the fullest extent," he allowed no alternative but to comply with the new approach. This is a dilemma for most leaders starting the journey, because we want to build consensus and use a teamwork approach. The problem is most teams will not accept lean principles by just talking about them. Ninety-nine percent of your organization will not start this journey based on talking about it; team members will have to get some personal experience in order to begin their own journey of lean learning. They have to experience the principles, and they may have to be "strongly encouraged" to get the personal experience that will lead them to a new view of how organizations can work effectively. No one on the team believes the core lean principles at the start. It will take about five years of deep experience before they will truly believe the core principles and practice them in their daily management.

Chances are, you will also have *antibodies,* people who are actively trying to derail your effort to change the culture (see Chapter 6).

Giving Your Leadership Team Personal Experience

You will find it necessary to *require* certain types and levels of engagement in order for individuals to begin to start on their own journey of new learning. And you do this by giving them the personal experiences with learning to see waste and remove waste. The place to start is with your leadership team.

When I started the lean transformation effort at HON/HNI, I required every business unit general manager to get at least twelve weeks of personal, full-time lean-event experiences in his or her first year as a condition of continuing in that role. When we started, most of them thought this was crazy. But now Danaher's executive immersion program requires thirteen weeks of full-time experience and learning about the Danaher Business System (DBS) for every business unit president and all of his or her direct reports. This level of experience for senior leadership is the only proven model for aligning senior leadership.

Today at HON/HNI, a similar leadership immersion process is in place. Those new to HON/HNI management roles (whether an outside recruit or an internal promotion) are required to get a structured set of four weeklong kaizen events in their first year. After that, they're required to get two more weeklong kaizen event experiences each year as a condition for remaining in the bonus program.

Something happens to a person as he or she accumulates these early kaizen-event experiences. One study found that associates' attitudes toward an organization improved significantly with each additional kaizen experience, continuing until it began to level off at a very high level after eight event experiences. Experience has shown that the impact of learning to see waste—personally—and then realizing how much waste could be removed in a week is transformational. Personal kaizen experience is the most significant building block for a successful lean transformation. At the same time, it is very hard to get senior management to realize that it is essential.

After you have an effort under way for senior leadership, look to build the breadth and depth of your foundation. The breadth will come from event experiences over a number of years for every member of your organization. This is how they get to the point that Toyota's Absher spoke of, where everyone in the organization acted like an industrial engineer.

It generally takes two events for team members to begin to believe that this "lean stuff" might be a good idea, three to seven events for a personal commitment to the lean philosophy to develop, and eight or more events to get the belief to a very high level. To take everyone up this curve may require ten years, so the important thing to keep in mind is that this commitment and growth in problem-solving ability is steadily growing as each member accumulates events throughout the organization.

Daily Improvement

Another fundamental approach to inculcating the lean culture is called *daily improvement* (the practice of daily problem solving, at the root cause, by everyone in the organization). I do not like to discuss this upfront, because when most CEOs hear about it, they immediately jump to the conclusion that this can be a shortcut to achieving lean results. The idea that some CEOs get when hearing about daily improvement is that all they really need to do is a little problem-solving training across the organization, and then simply ask everyone to improve every day. With any luck, by this point you realize that something this significant would not be that easy. In fact, achievement of daily improvement is the result of transformation and not an initial step.

Typically, it is best to initiate a serious focus on daily improvement after you have spent about two years spreading basic lean training and experience through kaizen events. However, daily improvement, like many of the Toyota practices, has more than one purpose and result. Daily improvement is an approach to pushing ahead on your True North metrics, but it is also a successful approach for accelerating a broad buy-in (culture building) of lean across the organization.

For example, at ThedaCare after several years of a steady kaizen event pace, management observed good improvement results and a number of people who were excited about where they were going. But not all the people—and perhaps not even a majority of the people—felt this way. Although ThedaCare had a fairly broad cadre of people who had built up significant problem-solving skills from their cumulative event experiences, it somehow needed to get everyone involved in improvement. The solution was to add a focused effort on daily improvement that would involve 100 percent of the organization.

The approach included four key building blocks:

- A one-day lean education program for 100 percent of the organization
- The establishment of visual management boards that highlight abnormalities in every area throughout the organization
- The implementation of 5S in every area throughout the organization
- The institutionalization of a daily improvement process based on problems that were highlighted in the visual management system and use of the basic problem-solving skills from the one-day training to address these problems

Similarly, at HON/HNI we instituted a Teian-style improvement system (see the Foundations section), built around standard Toyota practice, in our fourth year of the lean journey. This had the impact of broadening the buy-in while building broadly based, daily problem solving and daily improvement.

Challenging Your Team to Build Knowledge

Depth of knowledge is at least as important as breadth of knowledge, and you can get to some depth faster. Those who build deep experiential knowledge can usually accumulate about an event a month and will build their improvement skills to a high level in about three years, leading others in the process. In five to six years at this monthly pace of learning, those individuals will not only refine their knowledge of the tools and practices, but also be at a point where they believe the principles and practice them every day.

As this learning is taking place, you need to apply the ideas of challenge and discipline. You need to challenge your organization, and especially your leaders, to achieve double-digit annual rates of improvement in the four True North metric areas, while double-checking that these four core drivers are flowing through to the financial statements and aligning with strategic objectives. Properly applied, the challenge of significant True North metric gains and the discipline to achieve results through the process will drive the lean improvement activity. Keep in mind that there is synergy between substantial expectations for improvement and the activity of improvement. Success requires both activity and expectations for results and achievements. And you will find that meeting these challenges builds your people. Think about the overall culture, and the habits and values you want to build into your people.

As an example, one of the boards on which I participate is a privately owned firm called Watlow. After struggling with the initial issues in getting started on a lean path, Watlow undertook an effort to formalize the Watlow Way, its version of the Toyota Way, in conjunction with its sensei from Simpler Consulting. Watlow worked in a visual format, Toyota style. Now Watlow is working to align all associates' habits and behaviors with those it has identified as ideal in the Watlow Way. This is a journey that we all need to start—but that will really never end.

Figure 7.2 shows a model of the cultural end state.

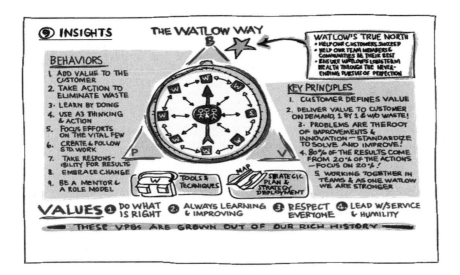

FIGURE 7.2
The Watlow way.

A couple of years ago, Toyota conducted a *hansei* (deep reflection) on where it was in its journey to build the Toyota Way within the North American business units of Toyota and its affiliates. Although there were many interesting lessons that came from this hansei, two stand out:

- It used the primacy of hands-on learning, the Socratic approach to teaching/mentoring (teaching through thoughtful questioning), and the structure of the weeklong *jishukin* event as a learning and implementation model.
- When summarizing the results of the hansei, Toyota asked the question, "What is the most common roadblock to the Toyota Way in North America?" The answer: lack of personal involvement.

SUMMARY

Building a long-term learning culture is the most difficult part of any lean journey, but it is also both the most powerful and the most personally rewarding part. As Kosuke Ikebuchi of Toyota has noted, "Westerners put too much emphasis on tools and technology, and not enough on philosophy and leadership behaviors." Building this lean learning culture can be—and should be—your legacy in your organization.

As a parting thought on culture, I have seen a couple of descriptions of a leader at Toyota. As usual, they are very focused descriptions that at first appear to be simple, but on further reflection reveal depth. Here is my favorite version:

A leader at Toyota should:
1. Possess a desire to lead, as true leadership is hard work.
2. Possess leadership ability, which is defined as the ability to get results through others.
3. Have a demonstrated desire and ability to mentor.
4. Possess a personal drive to pursue perfection [kaizen], through the Toyota Production System.

AUTHOR'S NOTE

At this point I need to thank the team at Simpler Consulting who worked with me to take our combined experience and observations and build the cultural attributes noted in this chapter. The outcome for Simpler is what it calls its tree, which is a model of the culture that it aspires to. See Figure 7.3.

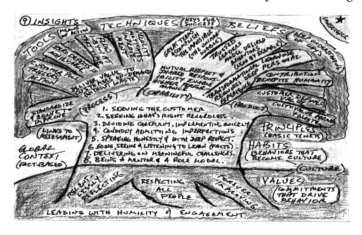

FIGURE 7.3
Simpler Consulting tree.

NOTES

1. Taiichi Ohno, "Evolution of the Toyota Production System" (unpublished manuscript).

Index

The Author

George Koenigsaecker is a principal investor in several lean enterprises. He is a board member of the Shingo Prize (the international award for "lean enterprises"), the Association of Manufacturing Excellence, the ThedaCare Center for Healthcare Value, Ariens Outdoor Power Equipment, Baird Capital Partners, Simpler Consulting (where he is also executive vice president), Watlow Electric Corporation, and Xaloy Incorporated.

From 1992 until 1999, Koenigsaecker led the lean conversion of the HON Company, a $1.5 billion office furniture manufacturer. During this period, his efforts led to a tripling of volume and culminated in HON Industries being named by *IndustryWeek* magazine as one of the "World's Best Managed Companies."

Prior to this time, Koenigsaecker was with the Danaher Corporation, where he was president of the Jacobs Vehicle Equipment Company (whose lean conversion is featured in the book *Lean Thinking* by Jim Womack and Dan Jones), and group president of the Tool Group, then the largest business unit of Danaher. In addition to leading the lean conversion of these operations, Koenigsaecker developed and implemented the Danaher Business System, a comprehensive lean enterprise model.

In addition, Koenigsaecker has held senior management positions in finance, marketing and operations with Rockwell International and Deere & Company. He is a graduate of the Harvard Business School.